Jobs to Jammies!

Jobs to Jammies!

GET OUT OF YOUR J.O.B.
&
BE A WORK-IN-YOUR-PJS ENTREPRENEUR

Bridget Brady

Jobs to Jammies by Bridget Brady
Copyright © 2017 Bridget Brady

ISBN-13: 9781977674586
ISBN-10: 1977674585

First Edition.

The methods described within this book are the author's personal thoughts. They are not intended to be a definitive set of instructions for this project. You may discover there are other methods and materials to accomplish the same end result.

The information contained within this book is strictly for educational purposes. If you wish to apply ideas contained in this book, you are taking full responsibility for your actions.

For information about special discounts available for bulk purchases, sales promotions, fund-raising and educational needs, contact Bridget Brady at AmpUpMyBiz.com or Facebook.com/AmpUpMyBiz.

Edited by Wendy Frado, EmpowermentStrategies.net

Cover and interior art by Jason Sikes, VillageGreenStudios.com

Acknowledgments

To the loves of my life, my brother and sister, Blaise Brady and Brooke Brady Wilkins, you have taught me the true meaning of unconditional love. I wouldn't be a fraction of who I am today without you.

Lois Brady, my mom, even when the world turns away from me, you always find a way to turn toward me.

Jason Sikes, my love, who designed this beautiful book cover, created all the interior graphics for this book, loves me and supports me like I've never been loved or supported, and is my rock, day in and day out, come what may.

My deepest gratitude to Wendy Frado, who is not only the editor of this book, but who kept me afloat so many times, and in so many ways, when my entire life seemed to be underwater.

Larry Broughton, who wrote the forward to this book, is one of my dearest friends, and who constantly inspires me in ways he probably doesn't even know.

T. Harv Eker, who taught me so much of what I needed to know to get out of my own J.O.B., and whose incredible programs gave me the tools to become an entrepreneur in the first place.

Craig Duswalt, who taught me the formula to get this book written, and who put me in the path of so many of my dearest friends.

Martin Presse, who took all my late night calls and questions, called me on all my BS, and always has something lovely to say about me.

Wendy Pasqually, who helps me remember who I am when I forget.

Coach and Scott Tomer, who founded the company with whom I started my very first business, and were there to lovingly watch me skin my knees as I tried to figure out how to be an entrepreneur.

Teresa Velardi, who was the catalyst for me to write this book, who said I could get this book done, and created a space for this book to be born.

Extra thanks to Mom, Brooke, and Diane Sikes, for their excellent proofreading. It's the only time I like it when you point out my mistakes.

And of course, Darby Brady, Teagan Brady, Hunter Brady, Chris Wilkins, Hadley Bay Wilkins, Amy Joanides, Jenara Prieto, Laura Ellis, Andrew Sherman, Becca Kendall, Lisa Stanley,

Heather Viau, Zander Cannon, Michele Mosler, and Lahoma Cronk. You may not think that you helped me write this particular book, but you are a part of my heart, and without you in my heart, this book would most certainly not be the same.

With great love, thank you all.

I dedicate this book to everyone who's ever heard the whisper,

"There is more than this, life is more than this,
you are more than this"…

and had the courage to listen.

Foreward

By Larry Broughton

At some point in every worker's life, there's the fantasy of leaving the time clock, shovel or cubicle behind to launch their own business and become their own boss. Increasingly, that fantasy is becoming reality for those who muster the courage to leave the rat race and seek a more joyful and rewarding path to success and significance.

With growing economic challenges and uncertainty around job security, each and every day more and more people launch their journey to work from home. For some, it's out of a lifelong aspiration for freedom. Others do so out of necessity as their traditional career paths fail. No matter the motivation, the dream of not having to get up and get dressed to make more money for "The Man" appeals to most of us! The allure of sipping coffee in our jammies, creating wealth and income at a pace that pleases us, and controlling our own economic destiny continues to drive the boom of home-based businesses across the globe.

Whether it's a full-time gig, or the chance to make some extra pocket change, the opportunity for online income and home-based businesses is growing by the day. As the number of exciting, legitimate opportunities grows, however, so does the number of scams, charlatans, and rip-offs. Thank goodness the book you hold in your hands is available as a road map to guide you, and help you navigate the minefields and quagmires that turn the journey of too many unsuspecting success seekers into the highway to economic hell.

As a natural skeptic, I wanted to learn the real story behind the passive-income-from-home phenomenon for many years. I finally made time to read countless articles and white papers on the topic, and then I interviewed dozens of home-based entrepreneurs who have made (and lost) lots and lots of money while working from home (and in some cases, quite literally, in their jammies!) So, based on my research, let me cut to the chase and answer the question, "Is it possible to make lots of money with a home-based business while in my jammies?" The answer is a solid, but qualified, "Yes!" But it won't be easy.

The legitimate businesses my friend Bridget Brady excels at, and coaches others toward success in, are exactly that: Businesses. These aren't get-rich-quick schemes. As with any other legitimate business, in order to find enduring success, it'll take lots of work. If, however, you follow Bridget's advice, you'll avoid trading time for money, and instead work hard now as an investment in your business so that you can reap significant benefits indefinitely.

As my contribution to your chosen path toward home-based entrepreneurship, let me offer you ten simple, yet powerful, tips

I've gathered from my research and interviews on this exciting journey:

1. **Groom yourself daily.** As tempting as it is to roll right out of bed and attempt to run your business, productivity will skyrocket when you start your day by simply changing your clothes (even if it means simply putting on *clean* pajamas). Brush your teeth, wash your face, and run a brush through your hair, and you'll find an immediate uptick in energy and focus.

2. **Identify a specific work area that promotes creativity.** I'm not suggesting you need to add an addition onto your home, or rent a larger apartment with an extra bedroom, but you should differentiate a space between your working life and your "home" life. Even if you identify an office nook, or convert a corner of the garage, you'll train your mind that when you are there, it's time for work, and when you leave the space, it's time for rest. Avoid working in bed, as the ergonomics suck for long-term productivity and wellness, and I prefer to keep that work energy away from my bed and retreat area.

3. **Be smart with your business and your money.** Create a legal entity for your business, get insurance, open a business bank account, and pay your quarterly taxes. On the personal side, since you won't have an employer taking care of the ins and outs of your 401(k) administration and retirement, develop a plan for savings and health insurance. There are several options to consider, so hire

a reputable accountant, CPA and financial planner to effectively manage your taxes and financial obligations.

4. **Develop a schedule and an effective to-do list.** If you're like most other high-achieving home-based business owners, you're going to find it way too easy to let the excitement of the new journey turn into 14-hour daily treks. Although there will be times when that's necessary, don't make it a habit. Schedule your time, as if you worked for a benevolent boss, and stick to it. At the end of your work day, shut the door to your workspace and take an emotional and intellectual break. Write every task down on a well-formatted to-do list with assigned action steps, status checks, and completion goals. Review the to-do list each day, and conduct the "4D Test": Delete, delegate, defer, or do it.

5. **Enjoy your freedom and flexibility.** Although the high-achieving home-based entrepreneurs I interviewed work normal business hours, they are also quick to take advantage of being their own boss. When their kids have a mid-day school activity, or there's an early afternoon ball game they're longing to see, they put it in their calendar and make it a priority. They don't guilt themselves over it. They choose to celebrate their newfound freedom, and when they get back to their workspace, they tackle their projects with vigor.

6. **Get up, get out and breathe.** I was surprised to learn that many home-based entrepreneurs begin experiencing mild depression and anxiety due to lack of movement, fresh air, and a periodic change of scenery. Consider that when you worked away from home, at least you had a daily commute

that guaranteed some exposure to the outside world. Highly effective entrepreneurs are those who start each day with a short walk, and who take short breaks throughout the day to get some movement and fresh air into their lungs.

7. **Become extroverted and schedule human interaction.** Avoid becoming a recluse! In addition to getting out of the house for fresh air and a change of scenery, it's vital to remain intellectually sharp and emotionally stimulated by surrounding yourself with bold and bright people. Each week, schedule at least a couple social interactions with friends (a work-out, coffee, lunch, or a hike); schedule several professional meetings (even if they're via video conferencing); and one evening engagement. Your best friends and confidants should not be computers, but other humans.

8. **Avoid over eating and constant grazing**. Keep healthy snacks on hand. Most home-based entrepreneurs I've met admit that this has been a challenge for them. It's too easy to go to the fridge or pantry when looking for a stress reliever or for a bit of inspiration. If you're not careful, all that extra income you'll be earning will need to go towards newer, larger pairs of pajamas and sweats. Healthier snacks will keep your mind sharp and aid in keeping focus, both of which will lead to increased productivity.

9. **Keep it clean**. Few people report feeling more joyful and more productive in a dirty, cluttered work environment than in a clean and tidy one. Most find it absolutely inspiring to start the day in a comfortable, peaceful, and organized space. Before you end each workday, tidy up

your work area; get rid of the trash; file your paperwork; and create a welcoming space for your arrival the next morning.

10. **Enlist a mentor or the support of a home-based business expert.** It's imperative that you enlist the support of a seasoned and savvy expert who has been on the journey before you. She'll be able to guide you toward the high ground, keep you away from the cliffs, and shorten your journey toward your goals. A great mentor will offer a combination of wit, wisdom, accountability and cheerleading. An awesome mentor will inspire creativity and ideas...and what's the lifetime value of one good idea?

Welcome to the elite class of world-changers, innovators, and legacy builders. This is going to be a rewarding, exciting, and sometimes, terrifying journey—and for most of us, we wouldn't want it any other way!

Now, go do something significant today. Go get 'em!

Larry Broughton

Larry is an award-winning entrepreneur & CEO; best-selling author; keynote speaker; leadership expert; and former U.S. Army Green Beret. For more information on Larry and his work, please visit larrybroughton.me, yoogozi.com and broughtonHOTELS.com.

Chapters

Intro

Hello you. Yes, YOU. You're who I'm writing this book for, after all. Are you in a job you hate? Do you feel like a slave? Are you tired of waking up early and coming home late? Do your kids know your day-care professional better than they know you? Are you tired of not having enough money? Are you tired of being tired? Are you bored? Do you feel like you're doing what you're supposed be doing, instead of what you'd love to be doing? Do you feel like most of your passion has been siphoned out of you little by little, day by day, while you're busy "doing the right thing" for other people? Are you tired of having someone else telling you when to come and go, what to wear, when to eat lunch, how long you have for vacation?? And…do you wish that you had the choice to wake up only when you're done sleeping each morning, and even wear your PJ's to work if you wanted? Then, yes, I am indeed talking directly to you. It's nice to meet you. I'm Bridget. In the following chapters, we're really just going to have a conversation. A conversation that can, and will, change your life forever.

Since we're going to be spending some time together, let me tell you a little more about me before we get into the nitty and the gritty. I am a woman who fiercely loves her family and close friends. I will stand in the fire any day of the week for the people I love (and have many times). I am an entrepreneur, singer, actor, speaker, trainer and author. I love to affect people in a profound way. I am committed to fulfilled loyalty. Not blind loyalty, or forced loyalty, but the kind of loyalty that makes your heart sing and empowers you to fulfill your mission in life. I believe in honesty, integrity, and freedom. My mission is to live in, and bring others, happiness, joy and fulfillment. I do my best to walk through this world as a blessing, and think I do a decent job of that most days.

Growing up, I often felt trapped in a life and a childhood that did not feel like mine. I spent hours upon hours in my room, in my backyard, and in my own mind, dreaming of the life I would someday live. A big, bright, shiny life filled with fame, fortune, love, comfort, and happiness. And so was born my dream of becoming a super-successful singer and actor. I also grew up PDP (pretty darn poor) and realized that was also not what I desired, and thus was born my dream of being wealthy. So, when I was 17 years old, I moved to New York City to attend the American Musical and Dramatic Academy. I moved there with a few suitcases, a couple hundred dollars, a student loan and a dream. By the age of nineteen I found myself living in a tiny broken-down apartment next to the projects on the upper-upper-upper west side (officially West Harlem). I was broke (and I mean truly, I-didn't-know-how-I-was-going-to-eat-every-day broke) and I applied for welfare and food stamps just to survive. I was working as many terrible/humiliating little jobs as I could find, all the while acting in lots of great little *super*-low-paying productions. And as happy as I was, in many ways, to be "living my dream" in New York City (acting, singing, dancing, and chasing that big brass ring), I thought there had to be a better way to live, to make money, and to go beyond barely surviving each week.

As fate would have it, I met an amazing teacher and mentor who suggested that I go into computer science. Although I had zero passion for this, I knew that welfare, food stamps, and dangerous neighborhoods were not for me, so I gave it a shot and took some computer classes. Well, lo and behold, I was good at writing computer code—who knew? By the time I was 21, I was working as a software developer on Wall Street. (Those two years of my life from Welfare to Wall Street is another book, which I'll write next, so keep your eyes peeled!) For seven years, I was a Wall Street girl by day, theatre girl by night, making a strong six-figure income, and by some standards living the dream. But between my job and my acting, I was working easily 100 hours a week and I was exhausted…all the time. I had no passion for my day job, and ultimately I felt like I was a slave to my job, my income, and my life. Again, I thought there must be a better way. A way to make more than enough money AND be happy. A way to make more than enough money AND live my dreams. A way to make more than enough money AND be the owner of my life.

So, I went on a journey to figure out how to make the money I wanted, have the time I wanted, and live a life I truly love. This is a journey I am still on today. That is really what this book is about: Living a life you truly love. Whether that comes from working at home in your jammies as an entrepreneur, keeping your job, finding a new job, or finding a different path to making money — it's about finding new ways to help you live a life you truly love, and of course work in your PJs if you want to! But this book isn't about my journey, it's about yours. We'll use mine as a reference point, to illustrate some good do's and don'ts along the way, but as I said in the beginning, this book is for YOU.

One other note: I am going to say some things that threaten your current way of thinking and being. I am going to invite you to move outside of your comfort zone. And several times in this book, I will ask you to stop, think, feel and write. I HIGHLY recommend that you do just that. (If you're reading this as an eBook, you'll want to grab a notebook for the writing exercises.)

It's cute and all to just read the book and see what you see, but it will be profoundly powerful for you to read the book, do the exercises, and change your way of thinking, being, and doing. Trust me on this. I promise it will be more powerful for you, and I am a woman who keeps her promises…so let's begin.   •

CHAPTER 1
Why Bother?

"An entrepreneur is someone who
solves problems for a profit."
~ PEAK POTENTIALS TRAINING

And So It Begins

I t's 6 AM. My alarm goes off, and I feel a familiar pit of despair in my stomach. I wonder if I continue to press snooze for long enough, will I no longer need to go to work today? Alas, I must get up…shower, hair, make-up, suit. Coffee, coffee, coffee. I'm at the edge of late, so I'll have to run to catch my bus. My heels are in my bag, as I run to join the other tired drones on the bus. I ride for an hour to spend the day doing something I do not love, with people I wouldn't necessarily choose to spend time with if they weren't in the cubicle next to me, to eat lunch at my desk, or I could go out, but it's so stressful to get back in time for my meeting, and (errrrreeeccckk—this is the sound of squealing tires as I halt this story).

This isn't my life…well, it's not my life anymore. Today, as the title of this book implies, I work at home in my PJs. Most days I wake up when I'm done sleeping. I exercise, make myself some delicious breakfast, write in my gratitude journal, and when I'm ready, I start work. My commute is 30 seconds, I don't have any make-up on, my hair is in a ponytail, I work with whomever I choose, focusing on projects that bring me joy and fulfillment, and *most* of the time, I love my life.

Honestly, I think the number-one reason to be an entrepreneur in some fashion is, to quote one of my idols, Aretha Franklin, "Freedom, oh freedom, yeah freedom, people say FREEDOM!" Please don't misunderstand me and think I'm implying that entrepreneurs don't work. In my experience, entrepreneurs often work "harder" than many employees. But the difference is that it's in YOUR time, on YOUR schedule, with YOUR rules. The difference is that when my niece was born, I could take two weeks off to fly to Colorado to be with her and my family. I didn't ask for permission, I didn't take vacation days, I just went. I personally am a work hard/play hard entrepreneur. When I work, I am diligent and focused and am constantly striving to provide more and more value in the marketplace and in people's lives. When I don't want to work, I don't. I spend time with the people I love, I go on totally unplugged vacations (no cell phone, no computer), I take classes, I sit in my hot tub, I go hiking, I read, I nap, I travel…you get the picture.

If you want more control of your life and your income, it's time to have your own business.

I would also like to take a moment here to talk about full-time vs. part-time entrepreneurs. If you want to fully transition out of a job you're not passionate about, you can absolutely do that. But even if you love your job, or you truly don't want to give up your job, you can still become at least a part-time entrepreneur in some form or fashion. Entrepreneurialism is not for everyone, but you won't know until you try. The extra money and time freedom it will afford you can be well worth the effort. Besides, you could find a new calling that might surprise you.

If you have a desire for more time and money freedom, if you want more control of your life and your income, then it's time to have your own business. That is where more time and money freedom come from. They certainly don't come from being a slave to a company or another person. So, if you're interested in being a full-time, or part-time, work-in-your-jammies entrepreneur, you'll find what you're looking for here. Let's get started! I can hardly wait! I'm so excited for you!!

CHAPTER 2
What's Stopping You?

*"Action is a great restorer and builder of
confidence. Inaction is not only the result, but
the cause, of fear. Perhaps the action you take
will be successful; perhaps different actions
or adjustments will have to follow. But any
action is better than no action at all."*
~ NORMAN VINCENT PEALE

In my personal opinion, the number-one thing that stops most people from pursuing their entrepreneurial dreams is FEAR. Well, you know what I say?? F**k fear. (What??!! I can't believe she just said that! Well, I did.) So many of us are fear driven. We are making choices, big and small, not based on what we truly want, but on what we are afraid of—what we're afraid of losing, what we're afraid of winning, the fear of working too hard, the fear of not working hard enough, the fear of doing it "wrong," the fear of rejection, the fear of what others think of us, the fear that we can't do it, the fear that we can.

Where in your life does fear stop you? Take a moment to look at your life and think about some of the things you REALLY want. Make a list of those things on the next page. After we have your list, we'll look at: How many of those things are you working toward right now? How many are you not? And what's stopping you from going after what you truly want in your life?

What do you TRULY want?

Write down what you *truly* want out of life. Don't worry, no one is watching, and there will be no grade at the end.

I want…

_____

_____

_____

_____

_____

_____

_____

_____

_____

_____

_____

_____

_____

_____

_____

_____

_____

_____

_____

_____

_____

_____

_____

After you've written down your true (perhaps secret) desires, I want you to put a happy face next to the things you're fully going after right now, and circle the things you are not fully committed to, or taking action towards, in this moment.

Now that we know what you want, I'd love to know what's stopping you. (I bet you'd love to know what's stopping you too, right?) So, take a moment, take a breath, maybe put your hand on your heart and feel into what fears and beliefs are really stopping you from getting everything you want. You may find yourself getting emotional here. That's ok. Our greatest fears and desires have emotion behind them, and sometimes they're easier to just ignore; it's high time we give them a voice so we can deal with them. I'll give you some examples to get you started...

- Laziness
- What if I spend my time and I fail?
- What if I spend my money and I fail?
- What if I try as hard as I can and I fail?
- What if I succeed...then what?!
- What if he/she won't love me anymore?
- What will my friends think?
- People will expect me to...
- I will expect xyz from myself.
- I'm just too tired.
- I don't want to work that hard.
- I don't think I can do it.
- It's too hard.
- I don't know how.
- I have too many responsibilities to follow a dream.

- That's not the way life works.
- Hardly anyone gets what they really want, what makes me any different?
- Etc.

What's stopping you?

_____

_____

_____

_____

_____

_____

_____

_____

_____

_____

_____

_____

_____

_____

_____

_____

_____

_____

_____

_____

_____

_____

_____

_____

_____

_____

_____

_____

_____

The more clarity
you have about
what you truly
want, the more
choice you will
have to make
changes.

All right, this is where we start. Do you think that if you really want all the time and money freedom in the world, you can have it if you're willing to do what it takes to get there? If not, you're not alone. Most of us are not encouraged to be independent, fearless, educated entrepreneurs. Most of us have been taught to get a good job, work hard, and pray our retirement will be enough to live on someday…if we live that long. I promise that you can learn new skills that will help give you the confidence to go forward powerfully. We'll talk a lot about this.

Right now, take a moment and look at the list of things you truly want, and the list of what might be stopping you. Did anything surprise you? Did anything peek its head out of your subconscious and scare you? Are there things (or people) in your life that you know are stopping you from truly living a life you love, but you're afraid to get rid of them? It's OK. In fact, it's more than ok; it's good. The more clarity you have about what you truly want, and what's stopping you in your life, the more choice you will have to make changes if you want. You don't have to make massive breakthroughs with everything on your list…at least not all at once. It's a process, and I'm here to help.

Here are a few principles we're going to start working with:

- Learn what you need to learn.
- Take action where action is required.
- Be still where stillness is required.
- Commit to moving through the fear.

The learning piece can be from classes, seminars, mentors, successful peers, mastermind groups, etc. (I'm going to make several recommendations to you on these throughout this book.)

Action is literally getting off your cute little assets and going to work! Make those important calls every day, turn off your television, do the things you're not in the mood to do, but you know will help move you forward.

And of course, stillness. Take time off, meditate, read, sit in the hot tub with friends, take an entire day off after every trip you take to re-acclimate back into your life so you're ready to fully commit back into your business.

Lastly, commit to moving through the fear. You will notice, my friend, I did not say move past the fear, jump over the fear, or ignore the fear. I mean take the fear by the hand and say, "C'mon, it's time to move. I know you're not going anywhere, so I'm taking you with me." If you take your fear with you for long enough, it will get bored and move on, because it can no longer control you.

When you employ all of these four strategies, your life and your business run smoothly and are in constant forward motion. Now, go back and look at each item on the list of what's stopping you and write down some ideas about what would help you to address each item, even if you can't see yourself doing those things at the moment. If you can't think of anything, find a friend who you trust and respect, and ask for their help. It is often much easier to see solutions for other people than it is to see them for yourself. Don't be afraid to ask for help and get some perspective from someone who's not so close to the issue. We'll talk about what to do with these ideas in the next chapter.

CHAPTER 3
Where Do You Start

*"The journey of a thousand miles
begins with a single step."*
~ LAO TZU

Simplify, simplify, simplify

You know what you want, you have some ideas about what's stopping you, and hopefully you have even more ideas about how to move past what's stopping you. It's time to take another step on the path. If you are truly committed to being an entrepreneur, and being financially free, the word of the day in this chapter is *simplify*. Oh yes, my friend, we are going to start by simplifying your life. I know it's a dirty word, you might not like it, and I most certainly did not, not at first anyway. So here's at least a little bit of comfort for you—you don't need to simplify forever, but I highly recommend you simplify for at least a little while.

I'm going to take a moment to get quite personal here with you, but I think it will serve you to know where I'm coming from on this. When I was in Corporate America, I had a paycheck coming in every two weeks, virtually no matter what. And I got a little complacent, or perhaps a lot complacent, when it came to money, savings, or any strategy about my financial future. I think on some level, I thought I would always have a decent paycheck coming in, and I was young, so I probably didn't need to "worry" about it all that much. I personally was also exceptionally gluttonous with my money. When I made $40,000, I spent $40,001. I thought I just needed to make more money. So I got a better job and started making $80,000…and spent $85,000. Now this is where it gets "interesting." I honestly thought that I just needed to make more money, so I continued to climb the corporate ladder, making more and more, $100,000, $130,000, $150,000, $175,000; I became increasingly enslaved to my job and my lifestyle, consistently spending more than I made. When

I made $175,000, I would spend $200,000. It was a never-ending cycle…until I was put into a kind of "forced" simplification. I was laid off from my fancy corporate job in 2010. I had already started a part-time Internet business (thank God) and now it was time to make some hard choices.

As you may remember, the economic climate in 2010 was not favorable for getting a job. So, after a few months of freaking out, crying, trying to get a new job…and crying and freaking out some more, I made a choice. I decided that losing my job was a message from the Universe telling me that it was time for me to go full-time in my Internet business. And so I did. As I said, I already had my business going on a part-time basis, but I went from earning almost $15,000 per month with both my job and my business, to bringing home only $1,000 to $1,500 per month total, from just my part-time business. At that moment, I made less in a year than I was used to making in a single month. As you can see, I needed to do some significant simplification of my life so I could survive long enough to take my part-time business and turn it into a full-time income. As you might have guessed, I didn't have savings. That just wasn't my style! This required a major life and mind restructuring.

Wants vs. Needs

The difference between wants and needs has never been clearer to me than it was in this moment of my life. Just for fun, here are some of the things that I used to consider absolute necessities: Facials, mani-pedi's, drinks with friends, going to the movies, wine, chiropractic, acupuncture, massage, going out to eat, going almost anywhere in the world I wanted, cable TV, take-out, fancy skin-care products, etc. Turns out these are not necessary to live. What!? Yes, it's true. Other things that are not 100% necessary are an excess of food, treats, coffee at Starbucks, and expensive make-up. In the majority of my life, I am completely transparent, so here comes a doozy of a transparency for you. During the hardest part of this time period, my grocery budget was $7 to $10 a week. There was a time when I would have told you that this would be impossible! But one carton of eggs, a loaf of bread, some nut butter, jelly, a bag of frozen veggies, and many packages of ramen noodles later, it turns out that it is possible. Not enjoyable, but possible.

I'm going to take a brief and important pause here to mention three things. One: Obviously this is not how I live today, so that makes it much easier to talk about it. Two: Do you see why I would suggest a more planned, and hopefully much easier, simplification of your life now as you venture into entrepreneurial bliss, rather than the kind of forced simplification that I have seen many people (including myself) have to make? Three: I am NOT suggesting that you live some super-simplified, ever-budgeting, scrimping life! Quite the contrary! I'm suggesting that if you can find empowering ways to simplify your life now, it will be much easier to become financially free. Then when you are FREE, and not enslaved to a job you don't love, you can work on becoming rich. And work on it in your jammies!

The myth is, "work hard to get rich and then you'll be free." I learned (mostly from teachers who know better than I, like T. Harv Eker) that if you work hard to get free FIRST, then you can become rich. Additionally, if you simplify NOW, you can put that extra money aside to help keep you afloat as you're making the job-to-jammies transition. I would venture a guess that if you really take an honest look at your spending, you could save 20–50% of your income this year by cutting out many of the wants and mostly spending on your necessities. I know that some of you are thinking, "You are crazy, girl!! I am done with this crazy-talk book." Remember, this is not forever; this is for the moment, to more greatly empower your higher goal of long-term financial freedom. Let's do a simple example. Let's say you currently make $75,000 a year after taxes in your job. If you're like most Americans, you might be spending even more than that per year by leveraging your credit. But what if we re-engineered that equation? What if you found a way to *temporarily* simplify your life, and live on $50,000 of that income, and put $25,000 per year into savings? I know it might seem impossible right now, but I bet you could do it if you wanted. Here's why you might want to: Many people start a business part-time to get it off the ground, and it can easily take at least three years for a new business to really take off, and get into substantial profit that you can live on. During those three years, while you're getting your business off the ground, you could have saved $75,000. (More than what you're now used to living on for an entire year.) Now imagine how you could choose to leave your job and go full-time with your business, if you wanted to. You would have contingency money, or money to make smart investments with. You may always keep your job, but again, now we're back to one of my favorite words, CHOICE. With a nice buffer in the bank, you could choose to go full-time in your business, and not have the stress and fear of losing your place to live, or your car, or your ability to feed your kids, hanging over your head. Once again, it's all about more powerful choices.

To help you with this, let's make a list! You now see how I love them.

First, make a list of anything you spend money on currently. Then go through that list and circle anything that is not an absolute necessity. I'm not telling you to give these things up...yet. (Or maybe ever.) We're just making a list so you are coming from a place of *choice*.

(Here's an example of things I've spent money on that are not necessities to get you thinking: Cable TV, new golf clubs, perfume, spa treatments, an iPad, going out to dinner, Starbucks, drinks with friends, Christmas presents, wine, new clothes, new shoes, designer bags, etc.)

_____

_____

_____

_____

_____

_____

_____

_____

_____

_____

_____

_____

_____

_____

_____

_____

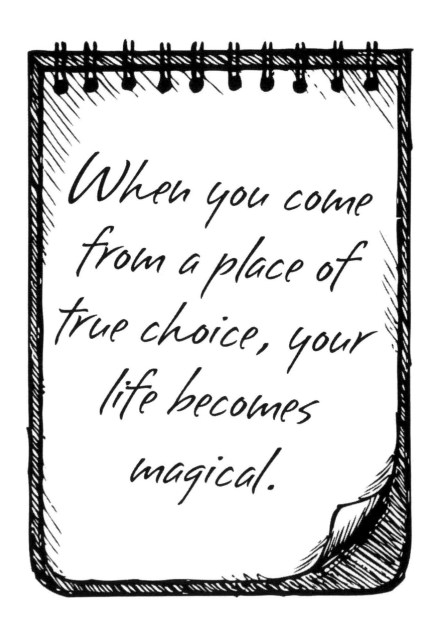

When you come from a place of true choice, your life becomes magical.

Now that we have this list, start thinking about small ways in which you can economize. You get to choose what changes to make, but I suggest that you start getting into the habit of considering every expenditure before you make it. Every dollar counts. This will feel very real to you when you no longer have a "paycheck" and your business is making every dollar. Again, this is not about coming from a place of lack or poverty consciousness, this is all about coming from a place of awareness and true choice. When you live most moments of your life from true choice, your life becomes magical.

Choose Your Vehicle

There are about as many options on how to be an entrepreneur as there are stars in the sky. And there are some great books already written about that. (See Appendix A: Bridget's Book Bag.) For example, I personally love making money using the Internet! I've had several monetized Websites that continue to bring me income every month; I own a full-service digital marketing agency, and I also teach people social media marketing and how to make money online, which brings me both income and a great deal of personal fulfillment. I also love online businesses because owning them gives me more time freedom. We'll talk much more about Internet happiness in chapter 5 (The Internet and Why I Love It). For now let's talk about some ideas on how you can choose YOUR perfect business.

If you already have a business that you love, then I say FOCUS. And by focus, I mean "Follow One Course Until Successful." I'm a huge believer in multiple streams of income, however it's also true that it's very hard, if not impossible, to start more than one business at a time. As a full-time entrepreneur, I now have several ways in which I make money: Social media management, Web and digital design, speaking, singing, teaching, training, writing, consulting, investing, and then some. I did not, however, start all of these income avenues at the same time! I got one business up and running, and at least relatively successful before I'd start the next. Which brings me to creating systems for EVERYTHING, and we'll talk all about that in the next chapter.

Now let's get real. If you have a business that you don't love, then I suggest you move toward having one that you do. (After all, if you're going to do something every day that you don't love, you may as well just go get a job.) You have several options. Sell your business. Ditch your business. Or, rethink and systemize until you like it a whole lot more.

If you don't yet have a business at all, or a business that you absolutely love, it's time to find one. There are so many great ways to make money, but we have been trained to think that a J.O.B. is the only way. I call it a J.O.B. to stand for Just Over Broke. Most people who just have a job as their sole source of income are indeed just over broke. Everyone on this planet who is truly wealthy either got wealthy with some sort of business, an inheritance from someone else who had some sort of business, or possibly is a celebrity. Now, if you do have a job that you love (the J.O.B.s I still love, and happily take, are singing and acting), I'm not telling you to give that up! On the contrary, keep those jobs and love them. Just don't be fooled into thinking that they will create sustainable wealth for you, which is the goal, or passive income (income that you make without trading your time for dollars, in other words the money you make while you are sleeping), which is one of the best tools to move you toward that goal.

As long as you are trading your time for money, you will never be rich. There is one finite thing on the planet, and that is time. No matter how much money you make for your time, it will not be able to create unlimited wealth, because there are only so many hours in the day for you to make money. Even movie stars and sports figures either need to leverage their celebrity status in other ways or invest their money in order to create sustainable wealth for the long term. How many people have we heard of who were once "rich and famous" and are now broke? In addition to that, typically when you stop working for any reason, you stop making money. This is not a good model for creating wealth or freedom. What I suggest for those of you who love your jobs, but want more, is to start a *part-time* business. Have an *additional* stream of income, and start getting comfortable with the idea of directing your own future. Besides, you never know when your part-time business will become your full-time business. I speak from experience. Way-too-many-dinners-of-ramen-noodles experience.

Some people know exactly what they'd like to do, and may have known for a long time. If you're still thinking about, and looking for your ideal business, read books, brainstorm, and talk to your friends who are in business now, as well as the friends who know you best and can help you figure out what you're great at doing. There are also numerous "tests" and surveys you can take that can help to remind you about things you enjoy that you would be able to build a business around. There are tons of turn-key businesses like franchises, network marketing companies, etc. that are ready to go for you. These businesses are usually quite easy to find. Go to almost any networking event, and there will likely be LOTS of people with home-based businesses to offer. You can also attend trade shows and expos that offer businesses for sale, like the "Work at Home Business Expo." In addition to that, there are entire seminars dedicated to showing off business opportunities. One I recommend is the "Never Work Again" course from Peak Potentials Training. Many of the options displayed there are plug-and-play businesses.

You can also start something from scratch! While many of us feel that we don't know the first thing about starting a business, that's ok. You have to start somewhere. You can find sample business plans in numerous places, and reading several of those will give you an idea of what you need to think about and do to plan. (Be sure to check out the recommended reading at the end of this book.)

Either way, the moment you stop trading your finite time for money, you can start creating financial freedom. This will take time, and that's ok, because at least you're getting on the path.

CHAPTER 4

I Love Systems

> *"Being busy does not always mean real work.*
> *The object of all work is production or*
> *accomplishment and to either of these ends*
> *there must be forethought, system, planning,*
> *intelligence, and honest purpose, as well as*
> *perspiration. Seeming to do is not doing."*
> ~ THOMAS A. EDISON

I have a system for everything. When I say everything, I mean EVERYTHING. My personal definition of a system is: A repeatable process that produces a measurable result.

Ultimately, you're an entrepreneur because you've realized that you want more out of life than just working for a living, right? You want out of being a slave, yes? Well, if you don't put some serious systems into place in your business, you will be just as much, if not more, of a slave to your business than you ever were to your job. You want to spend time working ON your business, not just IN your business. Here's what I mean: If you are the only person really working in your business, and you have to reinvent the wheel on every transaction, or every group of transactions your business is making, you don't have a business— you likely have a highly underpaid job. There will absolutely be times where you are working IN your business, particularly as you are becoming successful, but the more time you can spend ON your business, improving it, and growing it, the better.

Those who are really successful in a business and who also have a life outside of it have learned how to use systems.

Creating, Testing & Updating Your Systems
Take a moment to think about some of the tasks you do (or will need to do) on a regular basis in your business. Is there something that you are doing repeatedly? If so, chances are that you could create a system around that task that could make it easier, more efficient, and hopefully, less time consuming. Again, once you figure out how to do something once, if you build a specific

system around that task, it will often take you much less time and energy.

Here's an example: One of the tasks I used to have in my business is to take people on a virtual tour of different online tools for creating Internet income. For several years, I would do these tours primarily one-on-one. I would talk to each of my possible clients, one at a time, taking them on basically the same tour over and over again. So...same task, basically same talk track, repeated over and over. Sounds like it's time for a system! The first thing I did was to start doing my online tours with groups. So instead of one-on-one presentations, I started doing one-to-many presentations. This is the "testing" part of the equation. I took just one piece of the puzzle, changed that one piece, and then tested it for a while to ensure that the new way was still effective. Once I found that group presentations were just as effective as one-on-one presentations, they became part of my system. This helped me tremendously, but I was still spending a lot of time talking to people individually to schedule them onto one of my tele-seminars or Webinars. Now I needed to find a system for getting people to the presentations. One of my "golden" business rules is: If technology can achieve similar results as a human spending their time, use it! I talked to some industry experts and found a good program for scheduling people onto my tele-seminars and Webinars, and the next part of the system was born. Instead of doing all the scheduling myself, I let technology handle the scheduling. After a bit of testing, I found that this also worked quite well. But wait...there's more! Next, I trained others to do the same virtual tours I do, so that if I wasn't available, my business continued to grow without me!

If technology can achieve similar results as a human spending their time, use it!

I went from spending approximately an hour per prospect/ potential client, talking to them, finding a time to talk further, and doing personal presentations, to spending an initial five minutes with a single prospect/potential client, and then letting my system do the rest. I improved this system once again, and I now let my online presence, videos, and social media market-ing do a lot of the initial talking for me! This freed up a ton of my time to focus on making more actual sales, bringing more money into my business, and improving my other systems to continue to grow my business in a powerful way that requires less of my actual time. This is where I spend time working ON my business, not just IN my business. Of course I do both, but I allow systems and technology to do as much work for me as possible.

Another important note about creating systems is that you want to literally do the same thing over and over again, once you find the strategy that works. Keith Cunningham (über-successful entrepreneur), in talking about systems and the possible bore-dom of doing the same thing over and over again, says, "I'm bored, but I'm rich!" Once you're bored and rich, you can find plenty of ways to make your life more interesting.

When you're starting out, you may be afraid to even think of hir-ing others to work for you. Being the boss may require that you develop a different mindset and new skills. I suggest hiring peo-ple to help you as soon as you're able. If you don't have the bud-get to hire people, this can be done through professional trades, internships, or back-end points (in other words, a percentage of profits) in your business. There is an awful myth out there, which you may have heard: You should work on, or strengthen your weaknesses. This is a terrible idea! The much better idea as an entrepreneur is to strengthen your STRENGTHS, and delegate your weaknesses. (Check out Strengths Finder 2.0 in my "book bag.") Focus on and do what you are really great at; hire people to do the things you aren't good at, or simply don't want to do. I also recommend that you hire people to do any "minimum wage" tasks that take your time and energy away from your core strengths. Some examples of those are cleaning your own house, washing your own car, maybe even running your own errands. For example, let's say it takes you five hours to clean your house and do your laundry, and you can hire some-one for $150 to do this for you. Surely, you can find a way to make more than $150 in your business if you give yourself back those five hours. Additionally, you could spend those five hours with your family and loved ones. Time is your most precious commodity, and when put to its highest use, it creates more fulfillment in your life.

Here are some other examples of tasks I've handled by utilizing systems in my business. Use this list to help you come up with ideas for your business:

- Lead generation
- Sales calls
- Sales tracking
- Getting a new client started (we'll talk auto-responders later in this chapter)
- Training of new associates
- Sales presentations
- Monthly newsletters to prospects and clients
- Prospect follow-up

- Sales follow-up
- Packing for trips (I have a packing list document, so I don't have to *think* when packing)

Use the space on the next page to write down some ideas about what you can systemize in your business, whether you already have one or not.

Tasks in my business I could potentially systemize:

_____

_____

_____

_____

_____

_____

_____

_____

_____

_____

_____

_____

_____

_____

_____

_____

_____

_____

_____

_____

_____

_____

_____

_____

_____

_____

_____

_____

_____

Automation

Now let's talk about automation. There are several elements that make up the necessary day-to-day tasks of running pretty much every business. Those generally fall into the areas of: Marketing, administrative tasks, answering e-mails and phone calls, product development, making sales calls, leadership of your team or employees, following up with prospects, following up on outstanding invoices, customer service, training, etc.

If you have a business, we're going to talk about how to make it a lot more efficient. If you don't, think about a business you might like to start. Where can you utilize technology to make your life easier? If you're not very tech-savvy, you may need to talk to friends who can help you become aware of the tools that are available to you. For instance, if you're not well organized, you can miss out on business from new leads as well as from your established clients by not communicating with them in a timely and efficient manner. This means you may want to use: Auto-responders; customer relationship management software; event scheduling software; etc.

Auto-responders are automatic e-mails that go out to new leads when they opt into your database, or to existing clients when they are added to a specific list. Most e-mail marketing companies, such as iContact, A Weber, Mail Chimp, Constant Contact, etc., offer auto-responder functionality that is very easy to implement.

CRM or Customer Relationship Management software is a way to help manage your existing clients. There are fairly simple programs, such as ACT! or much more robust software like

InfusionSoft to help you manage and keep your clients and prospects engaged. CRM software helps you to do a multitude of tasks, including anything from keeping a database of your clients and prospects to reminding you when to follow up, sending out e-mails for you, or even handling more complex sales cycles and sending out offers for you based on programmed rules.

Event scheduling software, like EventBrite, can help you easily schedule and sell events to groups of people.

These are just a few examples, and there are fantastic new automation tools popping up all the time. All of these different technologies are quite easy to utilize and implement if you take just a little time to get to know them. If you are reticent to learn new technologies, stop it! They can help you in the long run. Just get out of your comfort zone, and don't be afraid to learn, fall down, fail, ask for help, and learn more. It takes some time to learn to use new tools, but once you know them, they will save you a ton of time. I promise.

In this day and age, much of any business' communication with clients happens online, so it's important for your business to have a well-considered and streamlined strategy for online communications. Let's first talk about getting someone to opt into your e-mail list, which is pure gold for many reasons. You will use this list to send information, sell products, let your clients get to know you better, provide value, invite people to events, etc. In the marketing game, she/he with the largest list wins. Once you have a large list, you can sell or promote almost anything, and there will be someone on your list who is interested. You can have someone opt into an e-mail list, mobile marketing list, or any other list that you can market from. In most cases, I recommend using what's called an "ethical bribe" to invite someone onto your list, meaning you give someone something of value in exchange for their opt-in (or personal information). This is something you give them for free, as a "thank you" for trusting you enough to give you their information. This could be a special report about your particular topic or area of expertise, an audio or video download, a discount they can use for a purchase, or perhaps a free conference call or Webinar within your area of expertise. The point is to give them something of value not only to say thank you for their information, but also as a little taste of what you do. The current paradigm of business is definitely to deliver value first, then ask for the sale.

Let's talk more about auto-responders. They are an important piece of your systemization puzzle. I use them whenever possible. For example, someone opts into your database. Do you want to have to go into your database to decide what to send to each of those prospects/clients one at a time? No, of course not! That would take up way too much of your time. I suggest instead sending an e-mail, or series of e-mails, via auto-responder; it's easy to set up a series of messages that will go out automatically after pre-set periods of time, so that each new contact gets the same communications on the same schedule no matter when they opted in. There are numerous e-mail marketing services available for a relatively low cost that make this incredibly simple.

When putting together your auto-responders, decide what information, and in what order, you want to send your new lead. If someone opted into your list, you now have a valuable prospect who has raised their hand and said, "Yes, please tell me more." Now you just need to decide what that "more" is. I recommend that the first thing you do is thank them. You have numerous "thank you" options. You can either send a simple e-mail, or put up a simple Web page that thanks them for their interest, and perhaps reminds them of what they are going to get. You could also put up a page with a link to the free report, video, audio, coupon, etc., that you promised them. You could then send them a page with a link to the next step in your information campaign.

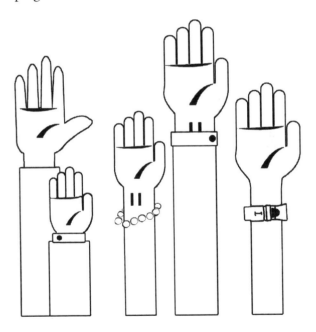

Some examples of next steps would be registering for your free or low-cost tele-class or Webinar, or watching a video. Perhaps visiting another Website to get more information, or whatever next step you'd like them to take. I am personally a fan of using a combination of these options. I love to offer people value in the form of a special report on my topic, e.g., The 5 Things You Need to Make Money Online, The 3 Secrets to Living an Authentic Life, The 7 Keys to Vocal Excellence. But instead of delivering these in one fell swoop, I prefer to set these up (via auto-responder) so that my new prospect gets one e-mail a day from me for a series of days. (In our examples above, 5, 3 or 7 days.)

This strategy provides both you and them greater value, and here's why: For you, you are now in front of your audience for a longer period of time, which not only builds trust, but allows you to give someone multiple opportunities to take the next step with you (whatever you've determined that next step to be). This also provides your new prospect with greater value because they have an opportunity to absorb the information in little bits and bytes. Unfortunately, or fortunately, we live in a world with an increasingly short attention span. The likelihood of someone being fully ready to comprehend and apply your three-to-ten-page report is low. However, the likelihood of someone reading one page at a time, one day at a time, and gleaning value from each page is much higher. This doesn't always apply, of course. If you're giving someone a recipe, you'll want to include everything in that first report, but perhaps you could give someone two or three recipes to get the same effect.

What does this look like in practice? Let's say you have five secrets or tips to share, and ultimately you'd like your client to register for a tele-seminar or Webinar. Here's how I'd lay out my responses:

1. Someone opts into my page with the "ethical bribe" of my 5 Secrets to XYZ.
2. I immediately direct them to a thank-you page that also gives them the opportunity to register for my Webinar.
3. Day 0 auto-responder (which goes out the same day someone opts in) is also a thank you e-mail, letting them know what they'll get and giving them an opportunity to register for my Webinar. (It's very easy to accidentally close a thank-you Web page, and if someone does, they'll be happy to get the e-mail as well.)
4. Day 1 auto-responder: Secret #1 (with the option to register for my Webinar if they haven't done so already.)
5. Day 2 auto-responder: Secret #2 (with the option to register for my Webinar if they haven't done so already.)
6. Days 3 through 5 auto-responders: Secrets #3 through #5 (with the option to register for my Webinar if they haven't done so already.)

My new prospect has now gotten to "know" me over the course of six days, and has actually had seven chances (including the very first thank you page) to register for my Webinar (my next step)—all without my lifting a finger, except to set up the auto-responder sequence just once in the first place. (You could also offer several options for a next step, just be sure to make only ONE next-step-offer in each email. A confused mind doesn't take action.) Again, systemize anything and everything you can. The less time you spend IN your business, and the more time you can spend ON your business, improving your knowledge and services, offering more value, and making more money, the better off you'll be.

Spend time working ON your business, not just IN your business.

Take a moment now to think about some of the things you could offer as your ethical bribe, and how you could deliver that value over a period of time. If you don't have anything ready to go at the moment, what information do you have just from living your life that others would like to hear? You can also use someone else's information, as long as you give them proper credit, and have their permission to use their intellectual property in this way.

Once you have as many systems in place as possible, in as many areas of your business as possible, you are now working smarter, not harder. And you are not duplicating work that has already been done, or can be done by technology or someone else.

CHAPTER 5
The Internet and Why I Love It

*"The Internet is a goldmine if you
know how to extract the gold."*
~ BRIDGET BRADY

Yay for the Internet!

Two of my most successful businesses are my current online marketing agency, and previously my Internet company, where I sold a variety of things online. Why, you ask? I'll be happy to tell you.

The Internet allows 24/7 global income. The Internet creates money while you sleep, vacation, spend time with your family, and hang out with your friends. Internet businesses can be run from anywhere on the planet with Web access. The Internet is freedom.

You already know that virtually everything either is, or is going, online. Shopping, travel, dating, information, marketing, communication, socializing and more. You can sell almost anything online. You can sell your products, or take advantage of affiliate marketing, where you sell other companies' products. (We'll talk more about that in a bit.)

Do you have to have an online business? Of course not! But I do recommend that you utilize the Internet as one of your money-making tools, and every business needs an online presence, so that people can find you and your services. Right now, however, I'm talking about more than just an opt-in page or an online brochure. I recommend actually having some products or services for sale on your site. This is the 24/7-income piece I'm talking about. If you have actual products for sale on your Website, you can literally make money while you sleep. This is where you're doing whatever you're doing in your life, and other people go to your Website, they click, they buy, and you make money.

So, what will you sell? If you have your own products, great— you can sell those! If not, I recommend doing affiliate marketing. You can also do BOTH, selling both your products and the products of other companies. I'm a big fan of "both" in many of life's arenas. I have personally sold both my personal products and other companies' products via my Websites.

Regardless of what you are selling, there are a few basic things you absolutely need to know. When putting up a monetized Website (meaning a Website that is set up for your 24/7 capture of incoming income) you have two basic options: Build or buy. If you have your own products, you will want to build a Website. If you're not a totally kick-butt Web designer, please hire one. You want your Website to not only look and feel professional, but you also want it to work. There are so many great Web designers around today, and many will work at a reasonable fee. Most Websites can be designed, developed, tested, up and running within a month. If you are on an extremely limited budget, you can also get started with a DIY Website, but I still recommend having a professional Web designer create a custom Website for you as soon as it's feasible.

There are almost infinite choices when it comes to making money online.

The other option is to buy an existing online tool. There are many fantastic turn-key, templated Websites that you can purchase for a very low cost. These Websites or tools are already pre-designed and developed for you. We will continue to explore these options as we go forward. There are almost infinite choices when it comes to making money online. You really just need to find the solution that fits your personal taste, aesthetics, and budget.

Affiliate Marketing

Affiliate marketing is the term for affiliating yourself with other companies and individuals to sell their products and get a commission or percentage of the sale. I am a fan of affiliate marketing, and here's why: You are *not* responsible for manufacturing, product development, fulfillment, shipping, customer service… or almost anything else in that arena. You can cut yourself into the distribution chain of hundreds or even thousands of vendors, market their products and services, and get an affiliate commission for doing so. Many individuals and large companies have affiliate programs. Some of the biggest affiliate programs for product sales are Amazon, Click Bank, and Commission Junction. There are private-label affiliate programs; you can also create affiliate relationships with other businesses.

Find a Way Regardless

Whatever your brand of Internet income, just get some! If you're not making money online, it's time to start. There are several classes, courses, tele-seminars, etc. (I know; I've taken them, and I teach them) that will show you different ways to make money online. (Check out some options I recommend at the end of this book.) As an entrepreneur, don't leave out this piece of the puzzle. This is a huge topic, and we could dedicate an entire book to this one piece. What I'll say for now is, go to some courses, classes, or calls; find the way that works for you, and add it as one of your strategies. In today's economy, leaving out Internet income is like deciding you're not going to drink water.

CHAPTER 6
Social Media Marketing

"Increasingly, consumers don't search for products and services. Rather, services come to their attention via social media."
~ ERIK QUALMAN

I t's a brave new world. Facebook, Twitter, LinkedIn, Google Plus, Pinterest, Instagram, YouTube…you name it. If you are offering a product, or service, or class, or seminar, or *anything*, it's time to make friends with social media. You can take entire classes on this one aspect of promotion. There are also entire books dedicated to this subject. My goal in this chapter is to demystify and simplify social media so that you can, at the very least, start reaping the rewards of this important tool. As a business owner, social media marketing is a critical component of your overall marketing strategy.

If you're over the age of 30, you most certainly remember a time when social media did not exist. If people "knew" you, they actually knew you. If you had followers, you called the police. Living by the extremely valuable rule that people buy from people they KNOW, *LOVE* and TRUST, social media gives you a platform to create a relationship with your audience and your clients.

Social media marketing is great for letting your audience get to know you a little better, adding value to the masses, and allowing complete strangers to become your raving fans.

Where to Start?

I recommend starting on three or four social media marketing sites, and becoming the master of those sites. There are new social media sites popping up every day. You cannot quickly master all of them, and you don't need to! That said, I suggest that you register your *name* or your *brand* everywhere! You want to own not only the .com of your name, brand, or business—you want to own your name everywhere you possibly can online. If you're not currently using social media marketing (SMM), get on as many sites as you can right away, sign up for an account and register your name. You may never use a particular platform, but if you ever do, you'll be happy you have your name. If you're not there now, start with the "biggies": Facebook, Twitter, YouTube, LinkedIn, Pinterest and Instagram. Again, anytime a new site pops onto the scene, at the very least register your name on it.

Now that you have an account, what in the world do you do with it? Well, let's start with the end in mind. What's your goal and what's your personal brand? (By brand, I mean: What is your title, tag line, and style that quickly and easily describes the value or benefit you deliver?) What is the end result you are looking for? Do you want people to become your clients and buy products? Do you want people to attend your seminars? Do you want people to become fans and attend your shows? Do you want a bigger audience for your radio show or blog? Do you want to become the recognized authority in your industry? What is it that you want to accomplish in a business sense? I know that many of you might use sites like Facebook for keeping in touch with family and friends, and that's GREAT! But now you're an entrepreneur, so you need to start playing a bigger game. When it comes to Facebook, you can certainly create a Facebook fan page. However, when you are creating your brand and your public persona, it's important to remember that people will indeed "cyber-stalk" you and read everything you have online, even all your personal stuff. We'll talk more about how to manage that in a bit. First, we're going to list what you'd like your SMM to accomplish for you.

Social media marketing is great for allowing complete strangers to become your raving fans.

What I Want to Accomplish with Social Media Marketing:

_____

_____

_____

_____

_____

_____

_____

_____

_____

_____

_____

_____

_____

_____

_____

_____

_____

_____

_____

_____

_____

_____

_____

_____

_____

_____

The 75/25 Rule

Now that you know what you want, let's talk about how to get there. In SMM you want the majority of your posts to be: Value adds; education; entertainment; inspiration; personal tidbits; etc. Thus, the 75/25 rule: *At least* 75% of all your posts must be valuable in some way to your audience, and NOT be trying to sell them something. This not only gives people a sense of who you are, but it gives them a reason to "follow" you and read your posts in the first place. Some people will even go as far as saying it's a 90/10 rule, but somewhere between there and 75/25 will suffice. Then *up to* 25% of your posts can be selling, making an offer, or inviting someone to a class, seminar, or Webinar you are hosting. Some great things to post in the 75 – 90% category are: Links to blogs or videos that offer value; links to value-adding recordings; entertaining videos that are relevant to your industry, brand, or personality; quotes by yourself or others; fun tidbits or anecdotes from your day; inspirational photos; branded memes; shared posts from other industry professionals you respect; and personal feelings that are ultimately congruent with your brand and/or image, etc. The 10 – 25% portion can be directly selling products and services to your audience or inviting them to events (live or virtual). As a business owner, the ultimate purpose of your social media marketing is to get people OFF of social media and ON to your Website, blog, content, and sales pages. Using the 75/25 rule will help you do just that.

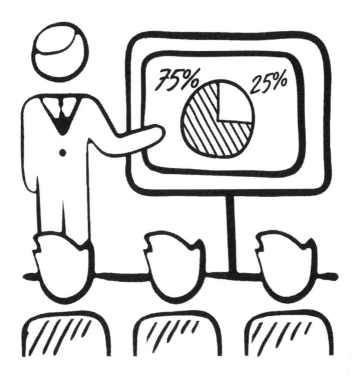

Let's Get Personal

Let's talk about what I mean by "personal" posts. I am not suggesting that you turn into some weird business-building robot who never posts things that are truly personal to you. That said, your closest friends can keep in touch with you in REAL ways. We still have phones and cars. I sincerely hope you have not reduced your personal relationships to SM and the digital world. The primary purpose of SMM for the entrepreneur is business—first, last and in between. So, you must, must, MUST keep even your personal posts on a relatively positive note, and congruent with the image you are promoting. People are making buying decisions based on your last post. So I'm not suggesting in any way that you should be fake—by all means, stay authentic; so few people are these days! I am suggesting that you tell the good, positive or empowered version of your truth at all times in social media. SMM guru Mari Smith says, "Don't post anything on social media that you wouldn't be comfortable having on the front page of the New York Times."

Remember also that when you post something on social media, you no longer "own" it. It becomes the "property," in a sense, of the SM platform you've posted on. Let me offer you some examples. Let's say you had an incredibly frustrating meeting with a client, or business associate. The "knee-jerk reaction" post might read something like, "Why are some people idiots and jerks?? If everyone just did what they said they would, instead of being whiny little babies, the world would be a much better place." Indeed, that may be how you feel in that moment…and it may even be true! My suggestion to kaizen (this is one of my favorite words; it comes from Japanese origin and means, 'continuous improvement') that post would read something like: "In business you will have good days and bad days. What I've found to be most important is to take focus off the good or bad, and put focus on what you've learned from each moment. Some lessons seem to feel much harder than others, but it's the learning we take with us. Please share one of the lessons you've learned in the comments below." Does that make sense? Same basic sentiment, but in a much more empowering package for your readers. Here's another example: Perhaps you're feeling down, or someone broke your heart. The thing you want to post might sound something like, "I have spent all night crying on my couch. Why, oh why, oh why doesn't he/she want to be with me?? Will I be alone forever??? Probably." Again, here's how I might kaizen that post: "The word of the day is trust. Today I'm simply sad, and am working on my trust. I will feel my feelings, and move forward, knowing that life can change in an instant, and ultimately love conquers all." You now preserve your online image, add something of value to your readers, and you are still being authentic, real, and vulnerable; you still get to say what you want to say.

How it All Works Together

Using the paradigm of mastering three or four (or maybe even five or six, if you're an overachiever like me) SM sites, you can have all of your campaigns working together to get to your goal. Let's say, for example, that ultimately you want people to visit your opt-in page and register for a free class, or perhaps purchase your book, video series, or a special report. On all your different SM platforms, you will continue to live by the 75/25 rule on each individual platform, giving away tons of value in 75% of your posts, and using that crucial 25% to drive "traffic" (online and off) to your specific goal. You also want to utilize all of the multiple platforms to continue to build your brand in a congruent way. Be authentic, add value, and stay congruent with your brand and message. One important note about your profiles: Unless you run a large corporation focused mainly on brand images, use pictures of YOURSELF, and when it comes to marketing, use the SAME picture (or two or three pictures) over and over again. You want people to feel like they are getting to know you. Not only is a picture worth a thousand words, but when they visit your Twitter, blog, YouTube, Instagram, LinkedIn, Pinterest, opt-in and Facebook pages, you want them to know they are in the right place, and connecting with the right person.

I Don't Have the Time!

The number-one complaint or fear I hear about starting a strong SM presence is time. And I agree, SMM can be such a ridiculous time drain, which we definitely want to avoid! When I first joined Facebook, I would spend hours just looking at other people's posts. I am certainly not suggesting that you spend hours a day on social media. Once you have your systems and accounts set up, you can absolutely have a fantastic SM presence with just 30 – 45 minutes a day. The trick, as in many other aspects of business, is to be consistent. If you are consistent about your posts to your chosen SM platforms, just 30 – 45 minutes per day can certainly bring you a ton of new business, new clients, and new cash!

Don't Try This at Home

Ultimately I recommend hiring a professional social media manager, or at the very least, taking classes on this subject. You don't need to spend thousands of dollars on SMM training! There are great classes you can take for just a few hundred dollars. I personally offer classes at AmpUpMyBiz.com, and I offer referrals to other trainers I recommend as well. As soon as you're able, hire a professional to manage your SMM, so you can focus on what you're passionate about, your business. In today's market, SMM cannot be ignored. Not only is it a powerful tool to grow your business, but it also has become simply a cost of doing business. If you're not on social media, you are losing clients, customers and income. My company does the social media marketing for many companies, individuals, and brands. If you're going to hire someone to do your SMM for you, you want to choose this person or company very carefully. You want to make sure that not only do they know what they are doing, but they can truly post in YOUR voice. If people don't feel like they are getting to know YOU or your company/brand via SMM, it has very little value. (Learn more about Social Media Management at AmpUpMyBiz.com.)

Ultimately, in today's economy, an effective social media marketing strategy is some of the best free and low-cost advertising you'll find, and its effectiveness builds over time with consistent use.

Additional Advertising & Marketing

Obviously, there are numerous avenues you can utilize to advertise, market and grow your business outside of social media. For example, T.V. and radio ads, newspaper and magazine ads, appearances on radio and T.V. shows, speaking engagements, etc. I know that we have barely scratched the surface of the sum total of all possibilities here, but these other media venues are outside the scope of this book. Therefore, I want to take a moment to recommend two of the best marketing classes I have personally ever taken: "The World's Greatest Marketing Seminar" taught by Peak Potentials Training, and "Rockstar Marketing Boot Camp" by Craig Duswalt. If you would like to delve deeper into the space of advertising and marketing, I recommend these courses as a great place to start! (Links to both of these courses can be found at the end of this book.)

CHAPTER 7
Speaking

"According to most studies, people's number-one fear is public speaking. Number two is death. Death is number two. Does that sound right? This means to the average person, if you go to a funeral, you're better off in the casket than doing the eulogy."

~ JERRY SEINFELD

P lease don't be angry. I'm now going to ask you to put on some clothes. I know...this book is called "Jobs to JAMMIES," not "Jobs to STAGES"! However, public speaking, speaking on stages—heck, speaking *anywhere*—is a phenomenal tool to build your business! This chapter is dedicated to ensuring that you don't overlook the powerful tools you already have: Your voice, your expertise, and your passion for your business.

This is yet another topic that could have (and certainly deserves) an entire book, or library of books. I want to give you some of the key elements to public speaking that can grow your business 100-fold this year!

Why Speak?

Speaking on stage, on radio shows, on podcasts, etc., is one of my all-time favorite ways to connect with more people. You have a business, or hopefully you will have one very soon. Do you think it would be more powerful to build your business solely based on one-to-one interactions, or would you enjoy one-to-many (meaning one you, but many prospects, customers, or clients)? Speaking can not only be some of the most fun and rewarding time you spend in your business, it can also grow your business and your income exponentially! When you are the speaker in the room, particularly if you are well spoken, and especially when you're speaking from the stage, you now have an incredible advantage. You are immediately positioned as an expert. You are given instant credibility on your topic. You now become the authority, the true subject matter expert.

When you're speaking from a stage, you are immediately positioned as an expert.

As the assumed authority, you will now find it much easier to make sales and get new clients and customers for your business! People will now seek you out in the room. This is a powerful paradigm shift in personal positioning for your business. It moves you from the energy of "I need to get out there and sell my goods and services" to "Yes, I am the authority on this topic. How can I be of service?"

Where Can You Speak?

Almost anywhere! One great resource is classes and seminars. Companies and organizations are already hosting classes, seminars, and boot camps about (or in some way complementary to) your area of expertise. I suggest contacting these organizations and getting onto their stages. This not only gives them more valuable content for their audience, but if you are allowed to make an offer (or sale), they often get a JV (joint venture) commission on your sales and make more "back-end" money during their seminar. (There are two primary ways to make money from trainings and seminars. "Front-End": This is what a student pays to attend the course, and "Back-End": Sales that come out of that seminar/class.) In addition to traditional classes and seminars, there are literally millions of organizations, networking groups and business groups who need speakers! All you need to do is connect with them. Let them know your area of expertise and tell them you'd love to be a guest speaker. You may be surprised by how happy they are to accept.

There are two basic compensation options available when booking speaking gigs. Once you are a known speaker, you can get paid speaking gigs, where you get paid simply for coming to speak. This will happen rarely, if at all, when you're getting started. Instead, most commonly you'll get paid through the ability to make an offer from stage after your training or presentation. Many organizations will allow you to offer your services, an upcoming course, training, book, DIY course, etc., in lieu of paying you. This is awesome! This not only allows you to give a tremendous amount of value by speaking for free, and helps you continue your personal mission, it allows you to grow your business through service to others. And when you get really great at selling from the stage, you will likely make much more money in sales than you would make from an up-front speaker fee.

I Promise You, It's Not the Words You Say

Let's talk about your VOICE. The number-one mistake I see most people making when it comes to speaking is putting way too much focus on their CONTENT, versus focusing on their CONTEXT. What I mean by this is that the way the words *sound* coming out of your mouth is far more important than the actual words you use. The *way* you deliver your presentation or training is just as, or even more important than, the presentation itself. From many different schools of thought, only 7% of what your audience perceives and learns from you is your data; the rest is visual and auditory. So what's a speaker to do? Your voice is your voice, right? Wrong. You can, and I strongly recommend that you do, train your voice. When you use correct breathing and speaking techniques, you will attract more clients, make more sales, and your audience will get a lot more value out of what you say!

I am lucky. I have been a singer and actor all my life, and have already spent many years and tens of thousands of dollars training my voice. It wasn't until recently that I realized the extreme competitive advantage that gave me in business. Did you know that, in most cases, your income is directly proportional to how well you speak? We've been honest with each other up to this point, right? So I will continue that now. I am going to highly recommend getting voice and speaker training, if you haven't already done so. If you're going to have the chance to speak on a radio show, or on a stage at an event, you want to be grounded, connected, clear, concise, well spoken, heartfelt, and amazing. In my experience, this takes training. Most people are not naturally gifted speakers. Some are, but most are not. And even if you have natural gifts, you can always learn valuable techniques and new ways to improve. If you're interested in speaking, find a class or teacher you love and study this skill set. Train your voice, and learn to become a master presenter and speaker. Consider this your personal (written) invitation to come to one of my live Vocal & Presentation Training sessions in Los Angeles, or at the very least one of my online training events. Training your voice and improving your presentations will empower every area of your business! Yes, obviously your presentations, demos, Webinars, tele-seminars, etc., but it will also help you at networking events, on the phone, in the boardroom, talking to prospects, and negotiating with clients and vendors. So give yourself and your business a huge gift; register for one of my upcoming courses at AmpUpMyBiz.com. In the meantime, I'm certainly not going to leave you hanging! Here are some of my top suggestions to get you on the path to becoming a master speaker and presenter.

Breathe

Whether you are speaking, selling, or doing any form of presentation, first, last, and evermore, you must BREATHE. I see so many people holding their breath during their presentations, and I doubt that they even know they're doing it. It sounds so very simple, but this is critical to your success in speaking. When you are holding your breath, so is your audience, or the person across from you, or even the person on the phone. They are feeling nervous and stuck and they don't know why. When you are breathing, and breathing properly, it opens up the energy of the presentation and the conversation. It also makes your voice sound better, stronger, and more powerful. Take the time to learn proper breathing techniques. Breathe fully into your rib cage and diaphragm, and let your voice initiate on your breath.

Breathing is also a fantastic way to calm your nerves, and it even helps you remember where you are in your presentation! When in doubt, nervousness, high emotion, forgetfulness, or stress, take some deep, grounded breaths. It will ground and center your energy, and ultimately help you deliver your message more powerfully...and make more sales!

Start Strong

The beginning of any presentation is when YOU are most NERVOUS, and your AUDIENCE is most SKEPTICAL. This could be an audience of one, 1,000, or 10,000. The formula is the same. The first five minutes of your presentation, talk, or demo is one of the most important factors to your success.

Be sure to have the first five minutes of any presentation carefully crafted with the following:

1. **Ground your feet, breathe and connect with your audience.** Do NOT, and I repeat, do NOT start talking the moment you hit the stage. This is most people's instinct, and it comes out of nervousness. Instead, walk confidently to the center of the stage/front of the room. Take a few seconds to breathe, ground yourself, and make eye contact with some of the people in the room. Warning: This feels SO strange when you first do it. I promise you will want to start speaking, laughing, saying hello…or engaging in some other nervous habit. Resist the urge, and take a few seconds to simply BE there with your audience. When you do, it is powerful!

2. **Enroll or engage your audience (by asking them enrolling/engaging questions).** An enrolling or engaging question lets your audience know two things: One, you understand them and their world; two, they are in the right place. For example, when I do speaker training I might ask, "How many of you have an important message to share?" "How many of you would like to make more money with that message?" This lets them know that I understand that they have something important to say, and I will help them monetize that message. I understand the world they live in, and I'm there to support and teach THEM.

3. **Acknowledge them for the time, energy and/or money they've spent.** Time is the only finite resource on this planet. If someone spends their valuable time and/or money to come hear you speak, be sure to acknowledge/thank them for that. People rarely get enough acknowledgment in their daily life. Treat them to some when they spend time and/or money with you.

4. **Welcome them to your program, tele-seminar, talk, etc.** Let them know the title of your program/talk/training and welcome them to it.

5. **Tell them a little about yourself to establish credibility.** This is the WHY someone would listen to YOU. Again, as an example, someone might know they want speaker training, but why would they want it from me? This is where I will tell my audience about my years of training, the specific things I did in my lifetime that make me an expert, and why they would want to put their trust in me to speak on and train them in that particular topic.

6. **Let them know what THEY will get out of your presentation, demo, etc. (Tune into everyone's favorite radio station, WIIFM, "What's In It For Me?")** This is KEY!! No one wants to hear what you have to say unless they know specifically what they are going to get out of it! I suggest keeping this simple and illuminating 3–5

specific benefits they will get out of your training/talk/ seminar.

When you master the first five minutes, it not only puts YOU at ease, it puts your audience at ease too. Now everyone can move forward together, on the same page, feeling connected to you and excited about what you have to offer.

Always Remember the 38%

As I previously mentioned, only 7% of perception is based on WHAT you say, and at least 38% is based on how you SOUND!! So many presentation and sales courses focus only on scripts and templates; that is only one part of delivering your message, or closing the deal.

Spend the time, energy and money to learn correct vocal production, including diction, enunciation, intonation, vocal variety, vocal placement, and resonance, as well as grounding and stage presence. I promise you that almost no one wants to hear what you have to say if it doesn't sound nice coming out of your mouth. Practice excellent diction, as well as rounding your tones so your voice is pleasing to the ear.

Again, if you haven't already studied vocal technique, I HIGHLY recommend it. If you are using your voice for your business, train your voice. The rewards will come back to you in spades! If you are a speaker, vocal training is critical. Not only so that you sound fabulous, deliver your message more powerfully, and make more sales, but also so that you keep your voice healthy and strong for years to come!

So…What Are You Supposed to Speak About?

So many people who want to come to my training events say, "I want to build my business, I understand that speaking would help me do that, but I'm not even sure what I'd speak about." YOU are an EXPERT. If you weren't, you couldn't possibly have a business. (Or I suppose you *could*…but it wouldn't be likely to do very well.) You may have heard that you should "write what you know." I say, "Speak what you know." Don't try to put together some contrived training you think people want. Here's a simple formula you can follow to easily put together a short presentation:

1. Think about what you are EXPERT in that would be of VALUE to others and that relates to your business.
2. Decide on three key elements, or data points, that you want to teach or speak about.
3. Decide on your next step. What I mean by this is: What would you like your audience to do next? Register for a program you have? Buy your book? Join your newsletter list?

Now that you know WHAT you're going to say, how do you say it? MOST speakers when given an hour to speak will get up in front of the room and "vomit" their information on their audience. MOST speakers are using mediocre vocal technique (at best) and think that we want to just hear them talk at us. The problem with this is multifold. One, it's BORING, and the audiences members' minds will wander, they will check their phones, and often not get a lot of value. Two, they will likely not retain most of what's said because they aren't participating. What we see and hear we tend to forget, what we say we remember, and what we DO we understand. The more you have your audience doing and participating, the more they will learn. Three, as previously mentioned, most speakers just get up and talk. If you want to stand out as a speaker, be in high demand, and make money from your speaking, I suggest structuring your basic talk/training in the following way:

1. Your "First Five Minutes" as previously discussed.
2. Data Point 1 (that you previously identified after deciding on your topic) and your message about it.
3. Exercise for the participants to DO around Data Point 1.
4. Partner Share: Have your participants partner up and share what they've learned.
5. Class Share: Give your participants an opportunity to share something they've learned with the entire class.
6. Repeat Steps 2–6 for Data Points 2 and 3.
7. Invite them to take your next step.

YES!! It is that simple. When you structure your training this way, not only is it fun and engaging, these are all accelerated learning techniques, so your audience actually learns more!

Serve Your Audience

This is your PASSION! Most entrepreneurs start their businesses because they are passionate about something, and when it comes down to it, most of us are passionate about serving, helping, or empowering others. Put your focus on serving your audience. It sounds simple, and it is. It is also tremendously powerful. Take the focus OFF of yourself, your content, your presentation, your technical gizmos, your hair, what you're wearing, and how you look. Put the focus ON truly being of service to whoever is in front of you. Not only does this make your presentation 10,000 times better, it also gets rid of those pesky nerves.

P.S. Speaking is FUN!! I know that it's supposed to be the number-one fear of most people on this planet. I promise that when you learn to speak and present powerfully, it can be not only one of the most lucrative ways to build your business, but also one of the most enjoyable ways to build your business. When you speak, you get to connect with and empower people in a way that few people on this planet ever have the privilege of experiencing.

I would like to give an extra thank you to both T. Harv Eker and Blair Singer in this chapter. Much of what I learned about training and the above formulas/templates I learned from these amazing trainers/facilitators. I have taken what they've taught me (as well as what I've learned from many other coaches over the years), made it my own, added my own special sauce, and have had the opportunity to train thousands of people. I always want to make sure I give credit where credit is due.

CHAPTER 8
Network Marketing

> *"One of the fastest ways to create wealth in this country today is through network marketing. Do what others won't do for three years and have what others can't have for the rest of your life."*
> ~ T. Harv Eker

Dirty Words

Network marketing, direct sales, MLM (Multi-Level Marketing), relationship marketing, you've heard all the words, and many people think of these as dirty words. If you LOVE network marketing, good for you! You and many wealthy people on the planet believe in the value of network marketing! If you don't like network marketing, that's OK, AND I invite you to open up your world and your mind, because it can be a wonderful way to create an additional stream of income. It's a wonderful way to create leveraged and residual income. It's also a wonderful way for people to start a business with very little initial investment. And the reasons you probably think you don't like it is because you've encountered people doing it badly.

Network marketing is NOT for everyone, but I invite you to take a look at some of the many positive aspects before making any final decisions.

How to Choose?

When looking at a network marketing business, there are a few key elements that I recommend you look for:

1. **Choose something you are INTERESTED in.** There are network marketing companies in a ton of different industries. Be sure to choose a product or range of products that you are not only interested in, but that you already use or would be happy to use. For example, if you love travel, find a travel company. If you love online shopping, find an online shopping company. If you love wellness, find a wellness company. If you love skin care, find a skin care company. Find something that is aligned with your values and interests.

2. **Find a company that has been in business for at least two years.** MOST direct sales and network marketing companies fail. Don't let this scare you. MOST new companies of any kind fail. The average life span of direct sales/network marketing companies is 18 months. So, as a general rule, if you find a company that's been in business for at least two years, they have a much better chance of survival going forward.

3. **Leadership and Company Founders.** Ideally, you want a company that not only has strong leadership, but also

has its original founders still actively involved with the company. If the founders are no longer involved, it begs the question…why? In any case, the leadership of the company calls the shots, so the more affinity you feel for them and their values, the more comfortable and happy you will be participating in the business.

4. **Lawsuits & Bankruptcy.** This is a concept that surprises most people. Most people might think it's good to avoid a company that's been through major lawsuits and/or bankruptcy. I say, find one that's been through at least one of those, if not both. Surprising? Here's why: Every successful company (networking marketing and otherwise) will go through trials and tribulations at some point. Many of those companies run into trouble and go out of business. If you are looking to build a huge business, leave a legacy, and create financial freedom through network marketing, you need to be sure that the company you're choosing is solid and resilient enough to come through a major trauma. If the company you've chosen has been through a significant "trauma" like a lawsuit, and they are still alive to tell the tale, this is a good sign of their stability.

5. **Mentorship.** Make sure when you're coming into a network marketing company that you will have great mentorship and great systems. I'm not saying to avoid registering under your sister, brother, or Aunt Sally. Definitely support your family, let them be your sponsor and work together! Just make sure that you have a dedicated, involved, professional up-line mentor who is

willing to teach and mentor you to the level of success you desire.

6. **FUN.** Network marketing, like any other business, can be hard. Really hard sometimes. Be sure that the product, company, and up-line you choose have an element of fun for you. If it's not fun (at least some of the time) you will quit. If the company, product, and system have an element of fun for you, you can become immensely successful!

Follow the Leader

On some level, network marketing is nothing more than an adult game of follow the leader. As with many of the topics we're discussing, there are entire books dedicated to this one subject. You'll find some of my recommendations in my "book bag" at the end of this book. So, without re-creating all the great books that are already out there, here are some of the key elements that have helped make me successful that many people, and books, don't often talk about.

Come From Your Heart

Everything is energy. This is true no matter what business you're in. People can absolutely feel your true intentions with every sentence you speak, every e-mail you send, and every phone call you make. I suggest truly coming from a place of service, being really authentic, and always coming from your heart. "Success through service" seems to be an especially important principle in network marketing. Your success is literally tied to the number of people you help to become successful. Much more on this in the next chapter!

Create Your Individual Brand

This can be a bit controversial among some network marketers, but I believe in it nonetheless. Your network marketing company simply provides the product or vehicle for you to utilize for your business. If you want to become a master at recruiting and building a team, I suggest creating your own individual brand. Get rid of all the "independent rep of…" cards. Decide who YOU are, and allow your company and products to support you. This serves two purposes. First, people can "smell" network marketers from a mile away, and you could have the ideal product for your prospect, but because network marketing has gotten such a bad "rap" over the years, that perfect prospect might not be interested…for no other reason than it's MLM. When you build your own brand, you have a much better chance of getting your product or service in front of more people. Second, if your company does go out of business, or if you choose to leave, you still have your personal brand intact. Now you can take your same customers and prospects and continue to offer them services and products separate from your company's products.

Come from a place of service, be really authentic, and always come from your heart.

System, System, System, System...Oh, and System

For network marketing to work, you must have a duplicatable system, not only for your down-line to use, but for YOU to use as well. If you are reinventing the wheel every time you add someone to your team, you are not only doing too much work, but you are losing momentum, and no one else on your team will be able to duplicate what you are doing. If you need to go back to the systems chapter, please do. Definitely find a system that works for you. (You can use a system taught by your up-line, or you can create your own, if need be.) Either way, find a system that works, use it, teach it, and your entire business can become as simple as lather, rinse, repeat. My personal version of this for network marketing is invite, expose, follow up.

Invite, Expose, Follow Up

1. **Invite someone to look at your business.** You always want this invitation to be based on something they may be interested in, and how your business could benefit them, while coming from your heart. Remember everyone's favorite radio station, WIIFM ("What's in it for me?")

2. **Expose them to your business.** Utilizing whatever system you have chosen, show them the value and benefits of your business.

3. **Follow Up.** You've heard this, I've heard this, and it is indeed true, "The fortune's in the follow-up." Oddly enough, no matter how much someone LOVES my business, they almost never call me to buy. It is when I call them to follow up that they make their purchase.

Why? Why don't they just call me if they're interested? To quote the great Jim Rohn, "I wouldn't take that class." I have no idea why, nor do I care. I simply follow up.

Does that sound too simple? Yes, it does. This is where most people get stymied in network marketing. They try to make something that is simple complicated. Don't. Follow the leader, come from your heart, and lather, rinse, repeat. Just follow a simple system that works. Again, and again, and again.

CHAPTER 9
Networking

"If you raise your energy, people
will be pulled to you, and
when they show up, bill 'em."
~ STUART WILDE

A h, networking. Many people, including myself, have a love/hate relationship with networking. Here's the thing…networking is an invaluable part of any business. That is just the truth. Here's why. Where does money come from? Other people. Money comes from other PEOPLE. There are many, many ways to advertise and promote your business. One way to truly grow an empire is to network, joint venture, and build relationships with other people. In this chapter we will talk about what networking is, what it isn't, and how you absolutely can learn to love it!

Verbal Vomit

Have you ever been to a networking or business event, and found yourself trapped, as if under a piece of heavy furniture, by someone attempting to sell you their product or service by means of vomiting their information all over you? Yes, I have too. I have taught entire seminars on networking, originally inspired by how badly I've seen people network. For now, you have this chapter, which, if applied, will change the way you network forever.

Let's start with the purpose of networking: Find the people who are looking for you, and provide value to them. (We will talk much more about this in chapter 10.) So the purpose of networking is for us to meet people, and appropriately promote our value, so that the people in the world who are absolutely looking for our product, our service, and us, have a chance to meet us. And vice versa—we might also find just the person or people we have been looking for to expand or grow our businesses. When networking is done right, it is a joyous dance, a pleasant and exhilarating energy exchange, where both parties come out better for it. Networking is also a learned skill, and an applied set of steps that will bring you a ton of success when used correctly and from the heart. So even if you are very shy, when you apply the principles described here, networking can ultimately become a joy for you. (Yes, really.)

Come From Your Heart

I have had the great honor of having many people who barely know me tell me what great "energy" I have. I believe this is due to many factors: Who I am, how I walk through this world, my intent, my transparency, my vulnerability, and my authenticity. I also believe that people can feel that I come from my heart. When I meet someone new, even in a business scenario, I do my best to make sure my heart is in the right place. I'm listening with my heart, speaking from my heart, and intending from my heart. When I'm at a networking or business event, do I want to promote, sell, market, and network? Of course! But how I do that is by coming from a place of, "What value can I add to this person's life?" And, "In what ways could my business truly help and serve the person I'm talking to?"

I have the great pleasure of Christmas caroling professionally every year. I sing almost seven days a week from Thanksgiving to New Years. I've done this for 15 years as of writing this book, and will likely carol for years to come. I absolutely la-la-la-love it! Not only is it a great "gig" for a singer, I also get to spread joy to literally thousands of people in the month of December. People laugh, cry, and their eyes light up with delight when they see us. You might be asking yourself, "How in the heck does this relate to networking?" We are spreading JOY, baby! We are coming from our hearts, and thus opening other people's hearts to happiness, and joy, and sometimes sadness—all *heartfelt* emotions. You may have heard that people buy people, not products; people buy with their emotions, not their intellect. This is all true. If you focus on your intention of bringing joy to others, all of this will come naturally. Think about something that you love to do, and work on bringing a similar enthusiasm to your networking events.

People buy
with their
emotions, not
their intellect.

It's time for another exercise!! (Yay!) Don't worry, it's not too scary and I'm not going to ask you to sing. Put your hand on your heart, actually your heart chakra, right in the center of your chest. Keeping your hand on your heart, close your eyes and take three deep breaths, focusing on breathing into your heart, putting energy and focus on your heart. (This is the time when you actually do it.)

If you cheated and haven't done it yet, do it now…seriously.

Now…do you feel the *lightness of being* that just brought you? Do you feel the softness that gave you? The light in your eyes may have just gotten a little brighter, and indeed, I bet your "energy" just got better. THIS is the secret to coming from your heart. When you are here in your heart, not in your head, people are naturally attracted to you, and are thrilled to give you their card, connect with you, and see how you can serve each other in a possible business relationship. You may want to do this exercise during breaks in your event to remind yourself of this feeling.

The Mechanics
I want to take a moment to talk about setting your intentions for each event. Some people go to an event with such unclear intentions, or worse yet, absolutely no intention for what they'd like to accomplish at the event. I'll give you a hint. Business events are not for "making friends." I feel that a clarification here is tremendously important, because I have met some of my very best friends at business events. Lifelong, best friends! But this was never my initial intention, it just happened through my staying open, being authentic and coming from my heart. Realistically

though, and for your greatest good, I think it's more powerful to set some clear *business* intentions for each event you attend. When you make friends, or find your spouse, that's icing on the cake. Some examples of event intentions are: Getting 100 business cards, meeting three new people who would like to partner with me in my business, finding $X in venture capital, selling X units of my product/service, learning xyz, meeting like-minded people to mastermind with, finding 10 people who are looking for exactly what I offer, etc....Very likely you will also find people who could be future friends, but that is not typically the primary reason you're going to a business or networking event. You're going to a business event to grow your business.

Let's get down into the nitty and the gritty—the networking "formula" that I've found works best. It's a three-pronged approach that, when executed from the heart, works incredibly well.

1. Get someone's card. Remember that networking isn't about handing out cards and running your mouth at other people. Networking is about making connections, and seeing how you can *serve* others. The name of the game, however, is getting and keeping the proverbial ball in your court. If you have someone's card, now no matter what happens next, you have their information, so you can follow up with them. Keep this simple. Just get their card.

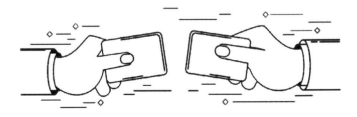

Example 1:

You: Hi, I'm Bridget, what do you do?

Them: I'm Andy, I'm a musician.

You: That's fun! I'm actually a singer, and am recording an album. Can I get your card?

Example 2:

You: Hi, I'm Bridget, what do you do?

Them: I'm Jennifer. I'm a pig handler.

You: Wow, I can honestly say I have never met a pig handler! That is really interesting; can I get your card?

Example 3: (To ensure that this horse is "dead")

You: Hi, I'm Bridget, what do you do?

Them: I'm Steven, I'm a dentist.

You: That's awesome! I'm looking for a new dentist. Can I get your card?

Does it seem too simple? It is. It IS that simple. Now you can continue the conversation, and get to know them better, but if they are called away, or get distracted, or you never talk to them again at the event, you have their card. This puts the follow-up ball in your court.

2. Find out what THEY are looking for. Now that you have their card, let's find out more about them and what they are looking for. Ask a simple question (notice I keep using this word simple). "Why did you come to this event," "What are you looking for here," "Who is your ideal client," or "What's the one thing that would really help your business grow right now?" The key is to get them talking about themselves and their business so you can learn more about them. How can you serve or help someone when you don't know who they are, or what they want?

Sometimes people will say things that don't entirely relate to your business or services, and that's ok, you're just getting to know them better. Once in a while people will literally tell you that they are looking for you. I was at an event several years ago, was meeting new people, making connections, and networking. One of the previous businesses I owned was helping people set up their own online travel business. I was talking to a woman at an event, and I asked her what she did, and she told me she was a nurse. Since I was coming from, and listening with, my heart, I noticed that there was a disdain and sadness in her voice when she said this, so I asked a follow-up question. "What's your dream? What do you want to be doing?" This is almost word for word what she said to me: "I don't really want to be a nurse anymore. I love to travel. My dream would be to start an online travel business." (I kid you not.) She literally told me that she was looking for me! By coming from my heart, I believe that I am better able to attract the perfect people to me.

During this follow-up questioning and conversation it also is possible to make someone a specific offer to purchase your goods or services right there and then. Yes, right there and then.

If someone says they are looking for what you have, you would be doing them a disservice to not make them an offer. To this end, it's great to have a specific "at-seminar special" or special offer that you are making at that event. Here are some examples you can use as a springboard to come up with your own "at-event" offer.

1. Today at this seminar, I'm offering two templated Websites complete with setup and one month of business coaching for just a $300 start-up.
2. During this seminar I'm doing one-hour massages in the evening in the hotel gym for just $50.
3. I'm doing an at-seminar special of a complete brand makeover for just $500.
4. I have an at-seminar special of a 15-minute interior design consultation for just $25.
5. I'm offering my Webinar series, The ABC's of Making Money Online, for just $97 for anyone who registers during this event.
6. I'm selling my new book xyz at this seminar for just $10.
7. At this event, I'm offering 10% off any social media marketing or Website packages.

Take a moment now to write down a few possible "at seminar" offers that you could make that relate to your business. This could be anything from a $10 e-book to a product or service that costs several hundred dollars. Just bear in mind that you will be making this offer primarily to strangers, or relative strangers, so you want to keep it doable for most people. Make it an entry-level price. I've found that anything between $10 and $300 works well; of course, consider who the attendees are at the event; if they're all wealthy individuals, you can sell something with a higher price tag. If you don't have a business, thinking about what this can be is a good way to help you plan what your business will offer. You're not going to necessarily make this offer to everyone you meet, but it's important to have this in your back pocket so you're ready to make the offer to the right people.

3. BAM-FAM. Book a Meeting From a Meeting. Now that you have a clear idea of your intention for a particular event, it's also great to have something to invite people to after the event. This could be almost anything that reconnects you with people who may be interested in what you have to offer. This could be a free tele-seminar, live event, Webinar, book launch party, or even an in-person coffee meeting with people who are a really great fit for you. I will purposefully schedule courses and Webinars for the week or two after an event I'm attending so I have something to invite people to. I will bring a registration form with me, so if someone is interested in the information, I can register them for a specific time and date while I'm talking to them. Again, book a meeting from a meeting. This gives you not only a specific time to reconnect, but also a great excuse to contact them after the event to follow up.

The Process Recap:

1. Set your intention so you know what you'd like to get out of each event. It's hard to get what you want when you don't know what you want.
2. Get a business card or contact information from everyone you talk to. This puts the follow-up ball in your court, where you want it.

3. Make a specific at-event offer to those who are interested in your business/service/product.
4. Book a meeting from a meeting. If someone is even remotely interested in what you offer, be sure to have a specific way/date/time to follow up with them again and show them more.

And with all of that...HAVE FUN! People are attracted to people who are authentically having a good time. If you find ways to truly enjoy the process of networking, meeting new people and growing your business, your business will grow more easily and the right people will be put in your path.

CHAPTER 10
Sorting vs. Selling

*"Selling is our No. 1 job. Never get away
from selling a lot of merchandise personally.
The more you sell the more you learn."*

~ JAMES CASH PENNEY

Mmmm...Sales. Delicious.

Do you hate to sell? Do you love to sell? I am going to welcome you to LOVING it! If you are an entrepreneur and you want to work at home in your jammies, you will have to sell something to someone to make a living. What I want to do in this chapter is demystify, de-blech, and de-fear selling.

I want you to shift your paradigm, and start thinking of selling as either SORTING or SERVING or BOTH. Many of you may have this idea of the "greasy" used car salesperson on the junker car lot who will sell his own grandmother for the right price. This is NOT the kind of sales I'm talking about. (No offense, used car salespeople! I drive a used car, and my salesperson was lovely!)

Thinking about your particular business or service, I want you to take a moment and ask yourself the following questions.

Do people need or want what I have?

Are people already buying these products or services from someone?

If so, why are they not buying them from me?

The answer to why you don't yet love sales likely lies in three elements:

1. You're not MARKETING your product/service/value.
2. You're AFRAID of selling and aren't promoting to enough people.
3. You're not ASKING for the sale.

Here's the real deal. If you have something of value, you can make a ton of sales and money; we just need to shift the way you're thinking of sales. Again, start thinking about selling as either sorting or serving. Let's start with sorting. There is a percentage of people on the planet who absolutely want what you sell, and you just need to find them. So you're SORTING the people who want your awesome product or service from those who don't. Then you just have to give those people who want what you have an opportunity to buy it from you. Ah, yes…it actually IS that simple. Important note: Not everyone wants your product or service. Period. Don't take it personally. The moment you start taking "no's" personally is the moment you slit your own sales throat. Much of the time it has little or nothing to do with YOU. Got it?

Not everyone wants your product or service. Period.

Don't take it personally.

Now let's talk about serving. If you truly believe that your product or service has value, then not only are you SERVING the people you show it to, but you are doing a grave disservice if you don't show it to everyone. Imagine how you can improve or even change someone's life with your service or product. Now imagine that you hide it from them because you're afraid to "sell." This serves no one, least of all you. I invite you to move your business from your head to your heart. When I'm marketing my business, I have such a strong belief in the value I provide that I feel like a big jerk when I DON'T share my business with people. This is why you need to be sure you offer something you really believe in. Sales is SORTING and SERVING. This paradigm shift will serve you well.

Features vs. Benefits

I find that many people try to sell their product by talking about its features rather than the benefits it provides. Let's determine the difference. A feature might be a monetized Website. Well… that sounds cool, kind of, but that doesn't really get the juices flowing. So, what's the benefit of having a monetized Website? Perhaps the ability to make money 24/7, even while you're asleep?! Now that's exciting. Another example might be shampoo that's sulfate free. If you know a lot about hair and shampoo that might mean something to you, but it's not a benefit. The benefit is that your shampoo will preserve the health and color of your hair. That's a benefit that people will buy. Ok… one more before we work on your personal feature/benefit list. Let's say you provide a meal delivery service. One of your features could be three prepared meals a day. Again…boring. But your benefit is that someone using your service could eat three super-healthy meals a day without ever having to cook. It's like having your own personal chef seven days a week. That is the benefit. Let's make a list of your businesses' features vs. benefits. Take a moment to identify as many features and benefits as you can for each business you have, or are thinking about starting.

Features vs. Benefits

Features   **Benefits**

_____   _____

_____   _____

_____   _____

_____   _____

_____   _____

_____   _____

_____   _____

_____   _____

_____   _____

_____   _____

_____   _____

_____   _____

_____   _____

_____   _____

_____   _____

_____   _____

_____   _____

_____   _____

Now that you know the benefits of what you provide, practice speaking about, marketing, and selling these BENEFITS, rather than just the FEATURES.

CHAPTER 11
There is Only the Tortoise

*"If you're not failing, you are not
moving fast enough, nor getting close
enough to your fullest potential."*
~ LARRY BROUGHTON

This Sounds Hard

I t is. It just is. I won't lie to you. I'd like to, actually. I'd love to say that it's easy to be an entrepreneur, and it's all rainbows and butterflies and unicorns; alas, it is not. There ARE some rainbows and butterflies and unicorns…and lollipops, and treats, and bubbles of happiness and accomplishment that will spring up inside of you like new flowers in spring. But not always. Sometimes you will fail miserably. That's part of how you know you're on the right track. So I want to talk to you about making all this work.

At this point we've talked about so many topics, strategies, tools, methodologies…but how do you sustain this? How do you put all of this together? How do you get up off your floor when nothing has gone your way, and you just want to quit? How does all of this actually work? This might indeed be the most crucial part of the puzzle.

Mindset

It all starts and ends with your mind. Thoughts are things! It is quite easy to want to give up, or even actually give up when things are not going your way. I have been there! When the cash flow isn't flowing, and your partners aren't doing what they said they would, and clients cancel, and sales are down, and the bills are coming in, and someone is mean to you, and to top it off, your love life is in shambles…If you are an entrepreneur, you will have days (or weeks, or months) filled with obstacles and disappointments. Assuming you're not going to actually quit… because you could. Quitting is a choice you have. It's not a powerful choice, but it is your choice. Remember, it's ALL your choice. But assuming you're not going to quit, what do you do?

I first suggest action. Action toward your goals is often a relatively quick way to change your state or your mindset. Do something. Almost anything. When you feel like you want to quit, and I promise that at some point you will want to quit, choose something to DO, and get into action. Write a blog post, set up some tweets, go to the gym, write a page of things you're grateful for, record a video, plan a party for your clients or team, send out an e-mail campaign, make a sales call, call a trusted colleague or mentor, just DO something. Do it with a heavy heart, but just do it. Now, here's my important caveat. I am not suggesting that you ignore or suppress your feelings. As a matter of fact, I HIGHLY recommend that you feel your feelings, and then take action anyway.

Might you need to spend an evening at the movies, having drinks with good friends, or sitting on your couch crying? For sure! (If you think I'm kidding, I'm not. Sometimes you just need to fully feel the hard, and the sad, and the hopeless. Fully feel it, so you can move through it, but don't get stuck in the feeling of hopelessness, or "This is too hard," or "I can't do this.") Take ACTION! Even a small action toward what you truly want goes a long way. You will find that it will help you feel better, and you are getting something done, so it's a double bonus. Take a moment and write down some specific action items that you can do toward your business and your personal goals. Then, when you feel the dragon of doubt creeping in, pick an action and start. Move that energy so it doesn't get stuck.

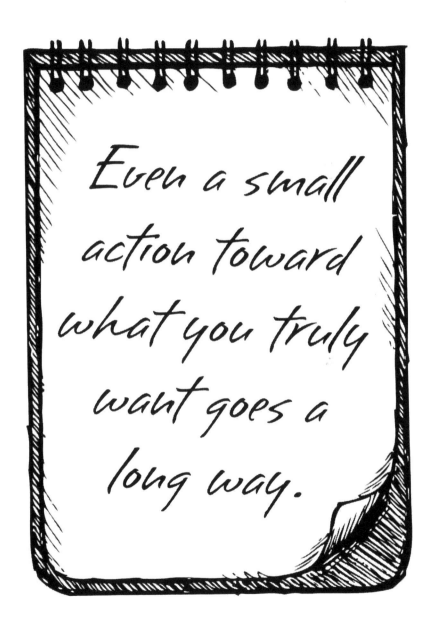

Even a small action toward what you truly want goes a long way.

Possible Dragon-of-Doubt-Slaying Action Items:

_____

_____

_____

_____

_____

_____

_____

_____

_____

_____

_____

_____

_____

_____

_____

_____

_____

_____

_____

_____

_____

_____

_____

_____

Balance

Another trap I've seen entrepreneurs fall into is having no personal life. Please don't do that. If you don't have the freedom to spend time with your family and friends and the people you love, if you don't have time to PLAY, what is the point? You might LOVE your business, and I hope you do; if you set it up correctly, you will. That said, be sure to take time for yourself, and do the things you love that are NOT your business. If you don't have the choice, time, or bandwidth to do fun, fulfilling things you love to do, you might as well go get a J.O.B.

There will, of course, be times, and seasons, where you mostly work, because that is what's required in that moment. Be sure to balance those with times when you don't work at all. It's all about balance. I am a work-hard-play-hard entrepreneur. When I'm working, I'm WORKING. I am a super-focused warrior who no one can stop. Then, when I go on vacation, I go on vacation. I unplug completely. I don't check e-mail or voicemail, and I don't work. I take the time to recharge my battery so I can return with laser focus.

Setting Up Your Workspace

I recommend having a specific workspace in your home that is your office. Ideally, you will have a separate office (a room with a door that is ONLY your office). If you can manage this, or set this up for yourself, I think this is ideal. However, if you cannot, I recommend setting up a space in your home, no matter how small, with your desk, chair, computer, phone, etc., that is ONLY your office. The only thing you do in that space is work. You can even get room dividers or a screen to further delineate this space. Here's why: When you work from home, it's very easy to get distracted with dishes, television, laundry, cleaning, kids, pets, projects, partners, clutter, and everything else that lives in your home. If you have an office, or an office space, that you condition yourself to WORK in, the distractions become much less powerful. Since I work almost 100% at home, a completely separate room that is my office is imperative for me. And when I'm in my office, I'm working. Equally as important, when I'm not in my office, I do my best to NOT work. This helps with that elusive balance that we just talked about.

Mind, Body, Spirit

Another piece of the puzzle is taking excellent care of yourself. I am certainly not going to tell you how to take care of yourself, but I am going to tell you to DO IT. I have found that the better I'm taking care of myself personally, the easier my business is, the better my energy is, and ultimately the more money I make. My recommendation in this arena is to find a spiritual practice and a health/fitness ritual that works for you. Then make yourself a priority, and take the time to take care of yourself every day. As entrepreneurs, we have so many things to take care of, and sometimes things fall through the cracks. Unfortunately, most often, the thing that falls through the cracks is ourselves and our self-care. We will spend hours upon hours taking care of others, our clients, our team, even our friends and family, but we won't spend an hour or two a day truly taking excellent care of ourselves. I invite you to really look at that, and dedicate yourself to a self-care practice that feels good to you.

If It's Not in Your Calendar...

It probably won't get done! The great part about being a work-in-your-jammies entrepreneur is that no one tells you what to do. The hard part about being a work-in-your-jammies entrepreneur is that no one tells you what to do! I highly recommend five specific strategies that will help keep you on task and increase your productivity:

1. **Keep a calendar/schedule.** Keep a well-organized calendar of your appointments and activities. Most people will write down their lunch dates, or doctor's appointments, but not their specific business activities. If you plan to make sales calls from 12–2 PM, write that on your calendar. Write down these critical activities, like sales calls, follow-up calls, social media time, etc. If they are in your calendar, you are much more likely to accomplish them.

2. **Find an approximate set schedule that works for you.** I like to have my mornings as my personal time. I like to sleep in a little, and do my own stuff in the morning; I like to have my "work day" from around 11–7 PM, with peripheral business activities (like writing blogs, or working on my book) from 7–8 PM. I, of course, schedule time to eat and rest appropriately during the day as well to keep my energy level up. Now here's the really cool part. YOU are ultimately in control of your schedule and could change your schedule every single day if you'd like. In addition to that, you might have an opportunity to speak, attend a seminar, or even play for a day that would normally be a "work" day. You are an entrepreneur! You can truly do anything you want every day…really!! And, what I've personally found is that when I find the groove of what I do MOST days, it's easy for me to fall right into that groove, and get my

work done. So find the groove you like! Find the timing that works best for you, and get in the habit of enjoying that powerful, prosperous, productive daily groove.

3. **Make a task list.** This can be done the night before, or in the morning before you start your day. The point here is to spend your time on and in your business in the way you choose each day, doing the activities that are truly most important to you. You can use any priority-setting methodology that you prefer, but here are the basics: Make a list of what you'd like to accomplish that day; identify the top priorities from that list; order those top priorities in a way that makes the most sense for your day. The point is to get the most important things done first, and if there is additional time for the additional tasks, great! If not, you've at least taken care of the big action items that will propel your business forward.

4. **Do a "money making activity" every day.** Especially when you are first starting out, you must be very aware of your cash flow. Unless you have an unlimited surplus of cash stored somewhere, you need to be sure you're making money, or doing what I call a "money making activity" every day. As we start out as entrepreneurs, most often we eat what we kill. Here's what I mean by that: No one is going to write you a paycheck because you showed up at work this week. If you'd like to eat, you need to "kill" something, or more accurately sell something, or do something that produces cash flow. Only you can determine what that is in your business, but it must be something that produces almost immediate cash. For

example, I love working on this book, but until I sell it, it's not producing immediate cash for me. It's still valuable for me to work on, and it will produce not only cash flow, but also greater opportunities, still I don't consider it a money-making activity. The opposite example would be sales calls. Sales calls are absolutely a money-making activity—calls that can lead to sales, which bring more immediate cash flow into your business. So, regardless of your business, especially at the beginning, be sure that you are doing something every day, or almost every day, that has the ability to bring money in the door.

5. **Swallow the frog.** I heard this at a sales seminar once, and love it…and hate it. Here's what I mean by "swallow the frog": Do the thing you most dread doing in your business FIRST thing in your day. If you dread your sales calls, do them first. If you dread follow-up calls, do them first. If you dread coaching your team, or sales meetings, or putting together your presentation, or writing your blog…do it FIRST. You have the most energy and resilience when you first sit down at your desk, not at the end of the day. So, do the "hard" things first, "swallow the frog," and the rest of your day will be a breeze!

Classes & Masterminds

Another entrepreneurial myth that seems to live in the minds of so many of us is that we can magically know it all, and that we can do it all on our own. You'll notice I used the word MYTH. One of the greatest things I've done for my businesses (and my life) is to take classes that support my business, and connect with other entrepreneurs in masterminds as well as in the world. If you've never been to a mastermind, it's a group of likeminded individuals who come together to serve and achieve common goals. Sometimes an expert in your field leads a mastermind, or sometimes a mastermind is equally led by your peers. Either way, if you find the RIGHT mastermind, it can be tremendously helpful for your business.

There are so many fantastic business-training programs that are available to us as well. (I included a list of my favorites at the end of this book.) The most important thing here is to find classes, training and masterminds that resonate with you, and/or are recommended by people you trust. Then…you must, must, must put the things you learn into practice. I've heard it said that "knowledge is power." I believe that APPLIED knowledge is power. Knowledge is mostly just knowing stuff, which will not make you any money. The bottom line is: Don't be afraid to invest your time, money and energy in valuable training. The most successful people know that it's imperative to keep learning.

You'll Never Really Make This Work Anyway…

Here is a frightening thought…some of you think I was talking to you as I wrote that last heading. Some of you have a little voice inside your head that says, "None of this will really work anyway. Maybe I should quit now, while I'm behind." That voice is NOT yours!! Do you know how I know that? You're reading this book! If you didn't think you could make this work, you would not waste your time reading a book about becoming an entrepreneur. That voice in your head is someone else's—maybe your parents', your spouse's, your friends', your teachers', the media's, your colleagues', etc. You must beware of the naysayers and the dream stealers!! I'm not telling you not to be realistic. PLEASE be realistic. Don't quit your J.O.B. before it's time. Don't fall victim to "magical thinking." Oh, you know what magical thinking I'm talking about. It goes a little something like, "I don't have enough money for rent next month, but I can take a trip, or spend a bunch of time hanging out with my friends anyway...I'm sure it will all work out." THAT magical thinking.

Be real, make a plan, work smart, do what you need to do, AND cut the negative people or the negativity out of your life. Stop the voice dead in its tracks. If it's a toxic person in your life, either have a conversation with them about shifting their attitude, or invite them to spread their negative energy somewhere else, just not with you. If it's someone you love who's bringing you down, talk to them about it, OR don't ever bring up your business dreams with them again. Protect your dreams and ideas like precious newborn babies. When someone tells you that you can't do it, in your mind, say, "Thank you for sharing," and move on. When YOU tell yourself you can't do it, say, "Thank you for sharing," and move on. Replace that negative BS with a different story. You are making it up anyway. Choose a story or a belief that empowers you. And when it gets really tough, call your "positive panda" friend and ask for a pep talk. They'll give it to you...that's what they do.

W.I.T.

Many people have said to me, "I just don't know how you do it." Well, here's my secret—you might not like it, but it's the real deal—I'm willing to do whatever it takes (W.I.T.) Especially at the beginning of this journey, while you're in the building phase, this may mean spending less on groceries, or going out less often with friends, or taking classes on the weekends or in the evenings instead of watching TV. In any phase of your business, this will most certainly mean going outside of your comfort zone again and again, and taking action in spite of your mood. And sometimes this might even mean taking a part-time job, or even a new full-time job to fill the gaps while you're creating your business, your vision, and your life. I know that I've vilified the good ol' J.O.B. a bit in this book, but sometimes that's what's required in the moment, if even for a short moment while you're building, or during downtimes. If becoming a successful entrepreneur was easy, everyone would do it. C'mon…who doesn't want to be able to work at home in their jammies?! But it takes a lot of courage, and hard work, and belief, all the techniques I talked about in this book, and more. And it most certainly requires being willing to do whatever it takes.

There is Only the Tortoise

There are no overnight successes. The overnight successes you hear about have been working on getting there for years! Many, many years—typically 10–20 years, or more! You just didn't hear about them while they were putting in the grunt work; you only found them once they finally got to the success part of the equation. All of these strategies take time to implement, and they also take time to work. I'm not suggesting that you don't push yourself, and take massive action, and work harder than you thought you could, and fall down, and fail, and get up again and again…and again. Do ALL of that…and know that the magical brass ring of entrepreneurial success may take longer than you think to attain, and will almost definitely take longer than you'd like. This is why I say there is only the tortoise. There is only moving forward, not quitting, putting in the work and continuing to learn day after day, month after month, year after year, and it will happen. One of my personal and beloved mentors, Juliet St. John, says, "The only way to fail is to quit." I've put my own spin on that: "As long as you keep going, success is inevitable." As long as you get the education, training, mindset, vehicle, etc., you need, you will be successful. You will absolutely have to make course corrections along the way, and adjust or even completely change things you are doing, but as long as you keep going, you will succeed. That's just the way it works.

CHAPTER 12
Get One Done

"I just get things done instead of talking about getting them done."
~ HENRY ROLLINS

Less Talking, More Doing

Wanna know something that people just love to do? People love to TALK about what they are going to do. Let me ask you this: Is there anything in your life that you would really love to do, that you talk about doing, and absolutely, someday, one day, you are planning on doing? Of course you do. We all do. Here's the problem. Until you've put the rubber to the road, until you've actually taken action on these goals, dreams and plans, it's very hard to tell how it's actually going to go. Beyond that, of course, it will never get done.

Let's take this book, for example. I talked vaguely, then specifically, about writing a book for about three years before ever writing one single word. I had ideas, I talked them over with people, I talked them over with myself, but I never actually started writing. Lucky for me (and anyone who gets value out of this book), the Universe had a timeline I wasn't aware of. A dear friend and colleague of mine invited me to speak on a women's tele-summit for thousands of women! She wanted me to talk about online marketing, being a successful entrepreneur, and working from home. Man oh man, was I excited! What an incredible opportunity to share my message and add value to the lives of thousands of women! There was only one small caveat, one teensy-tiny fly in the ointment. To speak at this particular tele-summit, I needed to be a published author.

Now, this wouldn't have been a problem if I had already written a book...but alas, I had not. Thankfully, I had a little bit of time, and a lot of motivation, so I told my friend that I would have my book completed and ready for advance sale by the tele-summit.

I will take a moment here to tell you that deadlines are your FRIENDS. Not only do I want you to NOT be afraid of deadlines, but if someone isn't making them for you, I want you to make them for yourself! If you don't know WHEN something will be done, it will likely NEVER get done. You can always move your deadlines if you absolutely have to, but having a goal as far as timing helps keep us moving. The result of the lesson in that example is literally the book you are reading right now. Pretty cool, right?

Deadlines are your friends.

If someone isn't making them for you, make them for yourself!

Let's talk about one more longer-term example, and then let's talk about the "one" that YOU need to get done. I had been talking about recording an album for over 20 years. If you've ever recorded an album, you know that this is no small task. For 20 years, I always had some excuse for why I didn't have an album yet. See if you've heard any of these excuses (or similar excuses) escape your lips or your brain: I don't have the time; I don't have the money; I don't have enough original material; I don't have the people I need to get it done; I don't have a recording studio; I'm not sure how the industry works; I don't know how to start; I don't know how to finish…sound familiar? Finally, I decided to put all those excuses aside, 20 years after first talking about it, and find a way to start making it happen. (Find my music at BridgetBrady.com, and on my social media!)

Now, I'm not suggesting that you jump into something you do not know anything about, with no research, no knowledge, and no clue. However, I think there's a popular myth that you need to KNOW EVERYTHING before you start anything, and this is simply not true. There are pieces of the puzzle you can start putting together, or classes you can take, or more importantly ACTIONS you can take toward your dreams and goals, long before you know everything. The truth is, you will probably never know everything about the goal you are working on, and I've found that we learn much more by doing than by talking about doing. Go back to the exercise we did earlier where you made a list of items that would help you to move toward your goal and pick one. You can continue building a map showing you how to get to your goal as you learn more about it, but you need to start taking ACTION. NOW!

Making Mistakes

This brings us to making mistakes. I'm going to offer you something really powerful right now, which, when applied with some basic common sense, will change your life. Are you ready? You are allowed to make mistakes. I'm going to say it again, just in case you missed it. YOU are ALLOWED to make MISTAKES. I think that half the reason people don't try new things, or follow their dreams, or live a life they love, is because they are terrified of making a mistake. I promise you, if you are doing things with your life worth doing, you are going to make mistakes. It's OK. When you are "getting one done," it's not the only time you'll ever do that thing…it's just the first time. You will: Make more than one phone call; start more than one business; do more than one grand opening; speak at more than one seminar; go to more than one networking event; have more than one Web page; order more than one business card; write more than one book; record more than one album; teach more than one class; talk to more than one person; make more than one sale; do more than one deal…you get the picture. We learn through our mistakes. As painful as it can be, we often learn and grow more from our mistakes than from our successes. Not always, but often. So, as an official fail-forward ordainer (yes, I just made that a word), I have officially ordained you with permission to make mistakes. This may surprise you, but most of the most successful people on this planet started on their path by learning as they went, and so will you.

So now that you know you don't have to be perfect, what do you want to get done? What are the tasks that you need to do to "get one done"? Use the next page to make a list. Here are some examples to get you started: Make a sales call; find a new business to start; have a client appreciation event; set up and send a social media marketing campaign; put up an opt-in page; write a book; write a song; write a blog; get a new client; have a grand opening event; call an expert; hire an expert; have a meeting; etc.

My Get-One-Done List:

*All the things large and small that I just need to do to "get ONE done"

_____

_____

_____

_____

_____

_____

_____

_____

_____

_____

_____

_____

_____

_____

_____

_____

_____

_____

_____

_____

_____

_____

_____

Now pick one or a few things on the list (depending on whether they are large or small tasks) and just DO them. Do them well, do them poorly, I don't care, just do them. Go ahead and make mistakes, just take action. Imperfect action beats perfect inaction every time. I promise you'll be glad you took that first step, made that mistake or had that huge success, and took that scary action and GOT ONE DONE. It is the small things that create the big things. It is the "slight edge" or the "compound effect" that creates the quantum leaps in your life. You are an entrepreneur, or you are about to be one. Embrace taking actions, large and small, comfortable and uncomfortable. Embrace taking action! The time is now. Your time is now.

IN CONCLUSION

If you really want to be an entrepreneur, it is possible. It will not come without sacrifice, or purpose, or intention, or failure, or good old-fashioned sweat equity, but I promise you it is worth it. It is worth it to be the king or queen of your own domain, the captain of your time, and the owner of your life.

As the hour grows late, and I write my book, or work on my album, or serve my clients, or market my business, it is almost always with great joy in my heart. So many people today spend life doing things they don't love, they spend entire evenings watching television, and they spend days doing what someone else has told them they have to do.

There is a prison in the world that keeps so many enslaved—the idea that we must keep jobs that don't make our hearts sing. If you have a job that makes your heart sing, for goodness sake, keep doing it!! If your heart doesn't sing, and your soul doesn't resonate with joy on a regular basis, find a way to create that for yourself. It's a daily practice; it's moment to moment, choice by choice, and breath by breath. It will not always be perfect. It will hardly ever be perfect, but you will be free.

Find a business you are passionate about or a business that is congruent with who you are, and go for it. Go for it now. Start NOW. Again, imperfect action beats perfect inaction every day of the week! It's ok to fail as long as you are failing forward. After learning from your failures, you will begin to create success. You just need to keep going. Take your own hand, be your own best friend, cry when you need to, reach out when you need to, get help when you need it, give yourself a good kick in the pants when you need it, and start NOW.

You may have heard this before, but life is not a dress rehearsal. Every day and every moment IS your life. Right now. Don't miss it. If entrepreneurialism is not for you, that's ok too, but if you spend the majority of your time at a job you hate, I promise you there is another way.

My greatest wish and prayer for you is that you will take what you learned from this book and make your life better with it. If you change even one thing that brings you closer to joy, happiness, and fulfillment, then I have done my job here.

I feel a certain sadness creeping in as this book draws to a close. I have loved this time I've gotten to spend with you—as much as, hopefully, you've loved spending time with me.

From the bottom of my heart, and the depth of my soul, I wish you all the best. I wish you every success and happiness that this life can offer you. Hopefully we'll cross paths someday on this fantastic road to living a life we love, living a life of our creation, and living the life of our dreams!

BRIDGET'S BOOK BAG

Secrets of the Millionaire Mind by T. Harv Eker

The Artist's Way by Julia Cameron

Young, Fabulous and Broke by Suze Orman

Put More Cash in Your Pocket by Loral Langemeier

The Alchemist by Paulo Coelho

The Four Agreements by Don Miguel Ruiz

The Slight Edge by Jeff Olson

Your First Year in Network Marketing by Mark & Renee Yarnell

The Road Less Travelled by M. Scott Peck

StrengthsFinder 2.0 by Tom Rath

Speedwealth by T. Harv Eker

The Art of War by Sun Tzu

FLASHPOINTS for Achievers by Larry Broughton

CLASSES, PROGRAMS AND TEACHERS
I PERSONALLY RECOMMEND

yoogozi Elite Private Mastermind
Larry Broughton
yoogoziMastermind.com

Rockstar Marketing & Entrepreneur Trainings
Craig Duswalt
RockstarMarketingBootcamp.com

Peak Potentials Training
SuccessResourcesAmerica.com

Live Out Loud
Loral Langemeier
LiveOutLoud.com

MORE FUN WITH BRIDGET

Book Bridget to speak at your upcoming events! Contact her through **AmpUpMyBiz.com.**

Work with Bridget directly—social media management, Website design and development! Study with Bridget by registering for her courses: Learn more about social media marketing and management; growing your business; improving your voice, increasing your sales and mastering your presentations! Visit **AmpUpMyBiz.com.**

Be sure to download her "Seven Simple Strategies to BRAND Yourself, BUILD Your Business and BANK More Profits" for FREE from the homepage.

Learn more about Bridget's singing and acting endeavors! Visit **BridgetBrady.com.**

Follow Bridget on social media and AMP UP your business!

AMPUPMYBIZ

AMPUPMYBIZ

AMPUPMYBIZ

AMPUPMYBIZ

AMPUPMYBIZ

THEBRIDGETBRADY

AMPUPMYBIZ.COM

ABOUT THE AUTHOR

Bridget lives and works in Los Angeles, California, with her beloved, in her jammies! She is extremely close to her family and dear friends. When not in her jammies, you will find her singing in the studio and at various venues throughout Los Angeles, Ventura, Orange County, and across the country, as well as speaking on stages all over the world. She's an avid scuba diver, world traveler, and lover of new cultures and experiences as well as people. Her love of empowering people to live their ideal lives is part of everything she does.

Made in the USA
Columbia, SC
14 October 2021